why SMART PEOPLE make DUMB CHOICES

DEBORAH SMITH PEGUES | **RICKY TEMPLE**

HARVEST HOUSE PUBLISHERS

EUGENE, OREGON

Cover design by Koechel Peterson & Associates, Inc., Minneapolis, Minnesota

Backcover author photo for Ricky Temple © Shannon Kuanfung

Why Smart People Make Dumb Choices
Copyright © 2010 by Deborah Smith Pegues and Ricky Temple
Published by Harvest House Publishers
Eugene, Oregon 97402
www.harvesthousepublishers.com

Library of Congress Cataloging-in-Publication Data

Pegues, Deborah Smith, 1950-
Why smart people make dumb choices / Deborah Smith Pegues and Ricky Temple
    p. cm.
Includes bibliographical references.
ISBN 978-0-7369-2852-6 (pbk.)
1. Decision making—Religious aspects—Christianity. 2. Choice (Psychology)—Religious aspects—Christianity. 3. Errors. 4. Emotions—Religious aspects—Christianity. I. Temple, Ricky, 1958- II. Title.
BV4509.5.P46 2010
248.4—dc22

                                                                        2010005751

Printed in the United States of America

10 11 12 13 14 15 16 17 18 / VP-NI / 10 9 8 7 6 5 4 3 2 1

CONTENTS

ACKNOWLEDGMENTS

Ricky Temple and I share a passion for teaching the practical application of God's Word with simplicity and directness. Therefore, this collaboration was a natural fit. His life balance, his receptivity to input, his wisdom, and his quest for knowledge are inspiring. People great and small are drawn to Christ through his kind and generous spirit.

During my 31 years of marriage to my beloved Darnell, he has faithfully supported my every endeavor. His adept biblical research, technical assistance, prayers, and patience make him a remarkable partner—for which I am eternally grateful. A special note of gratitude goes to the people who responded to our survey, shared their stories, or offered a prayer for this project. The input from Pastor Elvin Ezekiel, Regina Fair, and Crystal Kelley were invaluable. We are extremely grateful to our editor, Rod Morris, for his passion for scriptural integrity and literary excellence. Of course, the entire Harvest House team is an author's delight.

Deborah Smith Pegues

Great work never happens without a great team. My devoted wife and soul mate, Diane, has led my family support team for 30 years. My children, Ricky and Christina, are the wheels that keep me rolling forward with passion and energy. The staff and members of my church (Overcoming by Faith) in Savannah, Georgia, give me support that helps me achieve what I could never do alone. I am grateful for the hard work, patience, and editing/coaching skills of Nichole Palmer, a real champion who helped me hammer out my contribution to the project. Without question, my coauthor Deborah Pegues' insightful guidance has been invaluable. Every now and then, a person comes into your life that is smart, humble, and inspirational. Deborah's determination pulls you higher, her ability makes you humbler, but her friendship makes you better. It has been a pleasure and a great opportunity to share these pages with my friend.

Ricky Temple

INTRODUCTION: DECISIONS, DECISIONS

IT ALL HAPPENED WITHIN MINUTES. On January 15, 2009, Captain Chesley "Sully" Sullenberger, the pilot of US Airways Flight 1549 outbound from New York City's LaGuardia airport, would make one of the most important decisions of his life. On takeoff, a flock of birds got sucked into the powerful engines of his Airbus A320 commercial jetliner causing it to lose all power. The plane instantly became a glider. Air traffic controllers quickly concluded that Captain Sullenberger should return to LaGuardia or try to make it to another nearby airport.

However, based upon the speed and altitude the plane was losing, the experienced pilot knew this was not his best option. Rather, he chose to go for a crash landing in the Hudson River to the west of New York City. His plan worked. Everybody hailed it a miracle.

Testifying in June 2009 before the National Transportation Safety Board (NTSB), Captain Sullenberger explained that only the Hudson River was "long enough, wide enough and smooth enough" to put down his crippled jetliner.[1] His split-second decision was a smart one that saved the lives of all 155 people onboard. According to subsequent news reports, it was the first time in 50 years that a major aircraft crash-landed in the water and everyone made it out alive. His smart decision made him an instant hero.

In contrast to the Hudson River miracle, let's roll the calendar back about 20 years. On March 24, 1989, a little after midnight, the *Exxon Valdez* oil supertanker hit a reef in Prince William Sound near Valdez, Alaska, spilling almost 11 million gallons of crude oil over 1300 miles of pristine shoreline. A subsequent investigation by NTSB revealed that the shipmaster, Captain Joseph Hazelwood, left his third mate in charge, who improperly maneuvered the vessel when he allowed it to remain on autopilot during a critical passage. NTSB ruled that the captain failed to provide navigation watch, possibly due to his impairment under the influence of alcohol—or the fact that he was sleeping it off in his cabin at the time of the accident. Captain Hazelwood, obviously a man smart enough to have attained such a position, made a dumb choice. By his own admission, he drank "two or three vodkas" between 4:30 and 6:30 that same night. (Due to the mishandling of the evidence, he was later acquitted of drunkenness charges.) He became a villain and the butt of late night television talk show jokes.[2]

The accident was one of the most devastating human-caused environmental disasters ever to occur at sea. Thousands of animals and birds died in its wake. The spill had both short-term and long-term economic effects including the loss of recreational sports, fisheries, and reduced tourism. In the years that followed, various sea life showed shorter life spans. All of these consequences resulted from a dumb choice made by a smart person.

If these two examples are of too great a magnitude for you to relate to, perhaps some of the dumb choices below are more relevant:

- Rev. Hancock, a popular TV minister, is addicted to pornography but chooses to keep it a secret. Getting help is too risky. *Dumb moral choice.*

- Bob and Grace, unable to resist the temptation to purchase their dream home during their first year of marriage, sold the modest townhouse Bob had inherited from his mother and secured a loan with an introductory low interest teaser rate. When rates adjusted upward two years later, they could not afford the increased mortgage payment. They lost all their equity to a foreclosure. *Dumb financial choice.*

- John, a successful businessman, is absorbed with providing the best that money can buy for his family. He invests little or no time in building a relationship with his teenage sons who, resentful of their father's misplaced priorities, turn to drugs and alcohol. *Dumb relational choice.*

- Maggie, a 45-year-old social worker, discovered a lump in her breast. Not willing to face her fear of the worst, she refused to see her doctor. She died within six months. *Dumb health choice.*

The list of dumb-choice scenarios is endless. French philosopher Albert Camus said, "Life is the sum of all your choices." Indeed, wherever we are in our lives today is due primarily to the smart and dumb choices we have made.

What We Mean by *Smart* and *Dumb*

Throughout this book, we will define *smart* as "mentally capable of making a sound judgment in light of the circumstances and possible consequences." If you claim to be a child of God, we will assume that His Spirit dwells in you and has equipped you with the wherewithal to make smart choices. We will define a *dumb choice* simply as one "lacking sound judgment and forethought in light of the circumstances and possible consequences."

We want to caution you not to confuse *dumb* with *stupid.* Labeling someone as stupid cuts to the core of his inherent worth. Stupid implies that he is devoid of intelligence or common sense. However, we believe that dumb is as dumb *does.* Making a dumb choice is what you *do,* not who you *are.* Thus, you can choose to stop dumb behavior at any point. That's why we are writing this book—to show you how to make smart versus dumb decisions. In the pages that follow, we won't hesitate to share our own dumb choices and the related consequences. We hope you will learn from them. Fortunately, the grace of God has allowed us both to make many wise choices that have kept our marriages and our lives generally on track. We will humbly share those experiences as well. We'll also explore the human side of some smart biblical characters and their unwise decisions.

In an anonymous survey of our email community, 240 respondents shared with us the dumbest choice they have ever made. You're sure to learn some life lessons from their confessions and testimonies that we will weave throughout the book. Their names, as well as those of other contributors, have been changed to protect their privacy.

We will explore ten negative emotions that drive dumb choices, and we will reveal the seven secrets for making a great decision. We will show you how to engage in a critical self-interrogation so you learn to become your own objective counselor. Finally, we will explain how to apply God's Word—and thus His will—as you contemplate various decisions. Our goal is to give you the tools to facilitate wise choices so that you succeed God's way in your personal and professional life. The principles we set forth may appear to be simple, but they won't always be easy. Let's get started.

Part 1

REAL LIFE

CONFESSIONS
and

CONSEQUENCES

Chapter 1

DUMB MORAL CHOICES

"Moral excellence comes about as a result of habit. We become just by doing just acts, temperate by doing temperate acts, brave by doing brave acts."

ARISTOTLE

YOU'VE PREPAID FOR $20 WORTH OF GAS. Instead, the attendant gives you $25 at the pump. Do you pay the difference? You fought for a seat on a train, then a woman approaches with two children searching for a seat, but there is none. They stand next to you. Do you give them yours? A married coworker flirts with you. Your marriage has been a little rocky lately. Do you flirt back?

Morals. It's our personal code of conduct shaped by our conscience, values, societal and business mores, and our religious slant. Our sense of right and wrong influences our behaviors. Morals define our personal character and mold our convictions. In addition, morals are based on psychological values rather than physical or tangible effects. Therefore, morals color how we view life.

When I (Ricky) was 12 years old, my friends and I would stop at a neighborhood convenience store in Los Angeles for a honey bun pastry. I always paid for it, but this particular day, I decided to steal it. So with the stealth of a professional thief, I slipped the honey bun into my pocket and left the store. It was easy. It could have been the beginning of my life of crime except for one little thing: I felt horrible instantly. My mom had drilled into me that good people don't steal. However, my curiosity overruled my morals. My conscience, however, sucker punched me in the end.

For months, I avoided the store out of pure shame. Then one day I went back to pay for the item, but the store had closed. *Oh no,* I thought. *My act of thievery drove the store out of business.* Of course, this was impossible since the honey bun cost only ten cents. However, it was the principle of the matter. To this day whenever I am in the area, I drive by to see if that little convenience store has reopened so I can finally pay for that honey bun. Stealing was a dumb choice. This small incident had a huge impact on my life; I now have no tolerance for thievery of any kind.

> Some poor moral decisions can lead you down the slippery slope of deceit, ending with missed opportunities, destroyed dreams, and wrecked lives.

Are you living with the consequences of your poor moral choices? Ready for change? Let's look at others who have made similar choices. Then, we'll explore ways to strengthen your moral convictions.

Crossed Moral Lines

Anyone can make a poor moral decision. If he learns a lesson from that poor choice, it can prevent him from repeating the action. However, some poor moral decisions can lead you down the slippery slope of deceit, ending with missed opportunities, destroyed dreams, and wrecked lives. According to the wise words of Solomon,

> The godly are directed by honesty;
> the wicked fall beneath their load of sin.
> (Proverbs 11:5 NLT)

In our informal Internet survey, people told us how they compromised their values. It was interesting to read what some will confess when they can remain anonymous. Here are some of their responses:

- "My job sent me to a training class, and the instructor released the class early. Instead of going back to work, I went home and did not inform my supervisor according to company policy."
- "I decided to have an abortion; not just one, but two."
- "I met my first love at a hotel after 20 years to get closure because I thought I was dying or would die from cancer, and ended up committing adultery. Mind you—I had counseled other women in this area."
- "When I was younger, I joined a gang and did horrible things that almost led me to my grave."

These moral dilemmas are but a sample of decisions people make daily. It doesn't matter who we are or what we do. We all can make poor choices if we're not careful. Look at former U.S. President Bill Clinton. He had built his entire career on his astute leadership. He climbed his way from politics on the state level in Arkansas until he won the 1992 presidential election. According to his official White House biography, during his two terms:

> The U.S. enjoyed more peace and economic well-being than at any time in its history. He was the first Democratic president since Franklin D. Roosevelt to win a second term. He could point to the lowest unemployment rate in modern times, the lowest inflation in 30 years, the highest home ownership in the country's history, dropping crime rates in many places, and reduced welfare rolls. He proposed the first balanced budget in decades and achieved a budget surplus. As part of a plan to celebrate the millennium in 2000, Clinton called for a great national initiative to end racial discrimination.[1]

However, in 1998, he engaged in an indecent act with a young, female White House intern. Consequently, he became only the second president in history to be impeached by the House of Representatives. He was brought before the Senate and found not guilty. From that time until he left office, he received unprecedented low approval ratings. His behavior soured his reputation among many Americans because it is generally held that the president should be above moral reproach.

Over the years, Clinton has worked hard to rebuild his reputation. It's been a slow and arduous process, but because of his humanitarian work with the Clinton Global Initiative and his intervention in world affairs, he has begun to reshape a legacy that one poor choice almost destroyed.

Poor Moral Choices in Action

Not everyone gets a second chance. Sometimes you get only one swing of the moral bat. If you strike out, you lose everything. One couple during the formation of the early church who felt the fatal sting of moral failure was Ananias and Sapphira. After hearing the powerful preaching and testimony of Peter and John, the new church prayed for the boldness to speak the Word and for miracles to happen in the name of Jesus Christ. Following that prayer, the new Christians were filled with the Holy Spirit and a passion for becoming united:

> The apostles testified powerfully to the resurrection of the Lord Jesus, and God's great blessing was upon them all. There were no needy people among them, because those who owned land or houses would sell them and bring the money to the apostles to give to those in need (Acts 4:33-35 NLT).

However, Ananias and his wife, Sapphira, did not totally share the spirit of generosity. They sold a plot of land and kept part of the proceeds. This would have been fine if, when they presented their offering, they had said they were giving *only part* of the proceeds to the church. Instead, they told the apostles they were giving *all* the money.

So when Ananias presented the donation, Peter saw straight through his deception:

> "Ananias, why have you let Satan fill your heart? You lied to the Holy Spirit, and you kept some of the money for yourself. The property was yours to sell or not sell, as you wished. And after selling it, the money was also yours to give away. How could you do a thing like this? You weren't lying to us but to God" (Acts 5:3-4 NLT).

After Peter said this to him, Ananias dropped dead. Peter had several young men remove his body and bury him immediately. About three hours later, Sapphira arrived not knowing what had transpired. Peter asked her if the money she and her husband had given represented their total proceeds from the sale of the land. Here was her opportunity to tell the truth. But she refused. Peter caught her in the lie and she, too, died instantly. The same young men who buried her husband then buried her.

Reading this account always sends shivers up my spine and reminds me of the wise words of Solomon,

> Good character is the best insurance;
>   crooks get trapped in their sinful lust.
>   (Proverbs 11:6 MSG)

This couple died because of their selfish motive for giving and then lying to God about it.

Stronger Habits for Better Choices

Weak morals do not have to characterize your way of life. According to an article in the *New York Times,* a sense of right and wrong is inherent in our makeup as human beings:

> The idea that the moral sense is an innate part of human nature is not far-fetched. A list of human universals collected by the anthropologist Donald E. Brown includes many moral

concepts and emotions, including a distinction between right and wrong; empathy; fairness; admiration of generosity; rights and obligations; proscription of murder, rape and other forms of violence; redress of wrongs; sanctions for wrongs against the community; shame; and taboos.[2]

This goes along with what Paul wrote to the church in Rome:

> Even Gentiles, who do not have God's written law, show that they know his law when they instinctively obey it, even without having heard it. They demonstrate that God's law is written in their hearts, for their own conscience and thoughts either accuse them or tell them they are doing right (Romans 2:14-15 NLT).

Both of these statements indicate that we have no excuse for not knowing right from wrong because it's already in us to know.

This is the painful lesson golfer Tiger Woods learned. Prior to his much-publicized infidelity, he had earned well over a billion dollars for his prowess on the greens. But because of his moral missteps, he embarrassed his family and lost contracts with many of his sponsors. On his official website, Woods writes:

> I am deeply aware of the disappointment and hurt that my infidelity has caused to so many people, most of all my wife and children. I want to say again to everyone that I am profoundly sorry and that I ask forgiveness. It may not be possible to repair the damage I've done, but I want to do my best to try...
>
> After much soul searching, I have decided to take an indefinite break from professional golf. I need to focus my attention on being a better husband, father, and person.[3]

No doubt this was a hard statement for him to make; however, doing so demonstrates what we all must do when facing such dilemmas. First, he apologized for his transgression. Second, he acknowledged that his poor choice had damaged several relationships. Third, he vowed to try to repair what had been ruined. Finally, he removed himself from the environment that held the temptation.

When we find ourselves in such situations, this is the best course of action to take. However, if we engage in a little introspection, we may be able to avoid the mess altogether. The following questions can serve as a guide to thinking ethically:

- What benefits and what harms will each course of action produce, and which alternative will lead to the best over-all consequences?

- What moral rights do the affected parties have, and which course of action best respects those rights?

- Which course of action treats everyone the same, except where there is a morally justifiable reason not to, and does not show favoritism or discrimination?

- Which course of action advances the common good?

- Which course of action develops moral virtues? [4]

By asking these questions, we can avoid destroying reputations and ripping apart our relationships. We all have struggled on the fast moving waters of moral temptation. Often, the current sweeps us up and blinds us to the flood of possible bad choices. However, if we follow the steps above, we can make wiser decisions.

Chapter 2

DUMB RELATIONAL CHOICES

*"No man is the whole of himself; his
friends are the rest of him."*

HARRY EMERSON FOSDICK, BAPTIST MINISTER

HAVE YOU EVER STARTED MOVING in a positive direction when suddenly someone throws a monkey wrench into your life? Old friends and relationships can test you on every hand. Life philosophies and values you thought you had nailed down prove shaky. And to your surprise, you find yourself pushed into a sea of temptations you can't seem to resist. You begin to wonder, "What happened to all my values? How could I slide so far so fast from the things I say I believe?"

This is where Frank found himself one beautiful day in Georgia. He had finally made some smart life changes that reconnected him to his solid upbringing. He had a new job, a potential love interest, and new friends with better values. But on this breezy boring day, he decided to check on some old friends. These were not bad guys—most of the time. As he dialed an old familiar number, he felt a tug in his heart. Maybe seeing his old acquaintances wasn't such a good idea. When Frank was younger they had dabbled in crime—a lifestyle he had left behind. But Frank called them anyway. He found them at Harry's apartment and decided to join them there.

Once at Harry's place, Frank reminisced with his friends about some of the illegal escapades they had once engaged in. But with a little laughter and a smile, Frank tried to dismiss the memories. Suddenly one friend suggested they take that "ride" they had discussed earlier. "What ride and where?" Frank asked. They assured him it was just a ride. Frank wasn't sure. *But,* he thought, *these* are *my friends.* So when they left, Frank went with them.

A few minutes into the ride, Frank fell into a deep sleep. When he awoke 30 minutes later, he was alone in the car parked on the side of the road near the local bank. *I know they didn't go into the bank,* he thought. Just then, he felt that tug at his heart again and heard an urgent voice say, "Don't ask. Don't look. Just leave." Frank didn't take heed. He walked right into the middle of his friends robbing the bank. As they dashed out, he dashed out with them.

It's been 10 years. Frank finally has been released from prison. That day cost him his job, his freedom, community respect, and the ability to apply for a job without a prison-term explanation.

Frank's story is a common one among those whose lives have been damaged because of the relationships they kept. Sometimes the need to be with people trumps having a boring day. But not all relationships are healthy. As hard as this is to face, some people we associate with have toxic tendencies. In many cases, your presence in the relationship may elevate their lives or bring them cultural diversity. However, relating to them can be draining. They will fight to stay close to you because of the benefits.

> What binds people together is what they can get from or give to one another so their time spent together is mutually beneficial.

Meanwhile, the only benefit you receive is emotional or physical companionship.

But you don't have to be like Frank. You can make smarter choices. How? Understand that relationships influence all involved. Each person brings beliefs, values, thought processes, and core life philosophies to a relationship. The more time you spend together, the more those things change. You won't think, act, or believe the way you did before the relationship. That's why it's so crucial that you carefully consider the people you let into your life. Someone once said, "We control 50 percent of a relationship. We influence 100 percent of it."

Relationship Errors

You've heard the old adage, "Birds of a feather flock together." It means those who share things in common—for better or worse—usually end up in relationship together. What binds people together is what they can get from or give to one another so their time spent together is mutually beneficial. If there is no mutual benefit, there is no relationship.

However, some relationships unknowingly were built upon deficient foundations. The reasons for the alliances were never explored, analyzed, or their long-term effects even questioned. If you want stronger, healthier relationships, you must change the following habits.

Choosing People for the Wrong Reasons

When we were children, we gave little thought to how we formed relationships with those who liked the things we liked. We simply played together, ate together, and sometimes spent the night in each others' homes. We wanted them to laugh with us, listen to us, and be nice. It was all about what we had in common and what that person had to add to our lives. Our relationships were self-focused. We never really considered other criteria.

As we got older, we became more selective about those we called friends based on past experiences, life philosophies, and core values. We may have even created relationship categories: spouse, family, friends, associates, business partners, organization members. And though we've grown older, sometimes the process by which we choose people to be in our lives is still based upon what we learned as children. Therein lies the danger. Choosing people to be in our lives should be based upon common beliefs, core values, and morals. Allowing someone in your life who doesn't share these things invites heartache. Scripture says, "Can two walk together, unless they are agreed?" (Amos 3:3). And without agreement, a healthy, mutually satisfying relationship is unattainable.

Refusing to Ask Critical Questions

We need to take inventory of our relationships and ask critical questions such as:

- Is this person compatible with my beliefs and core values?
- Can he be accountable for his actions in the relationship?
- Does she know how to manage her emotions?
- Can we communicate effectively?
- Will this person be mentally, emotionally, physically, and spiritually available?

Asking questions allows us to see beyond the initial attraction and critically analyze the potential life consequences from being in relationship with a person.

Compromising Core Values and Beliefs

Remember Frank and his boring day? The moment he got involved with his old cronies he compromised his new core beliefs and values. The consequences of ignoring character flaws can be detrimental. Check out a few examples from real people who responded to our survey:

- Jane married the same type of abusive man—three times.
- Andrew married a woman without talking to God first. Now, he feels stuck because of the children and the years he put into the marriage.
- For four years Shauna allowed a college boyfriend to entice her away from her core values and beliefs. Her relationship naïveté delayed her educational pursuits.
- Doris kicked her cheating husband out of the house. When she let him come home, he cheated on her again. This time when she kicked him out, he left her as a single mother.
- Charles married a drug addict.

The people in these real-life stories all have something in common—they ignored destructive character flaws and compromised their beliefs just to have someone in their lives.

Sabotaging the Relationship

Then there are things we do to undermine our relationships. Sometimes we justify these behaviors as being "just the way we are." Unfortunately, that line of thinking flies in the face of reality. Think about it: If you are dishonest, why do you expect others to tell *you* the truth? If you are habitually unfaithful and lack self-control, why do you think your spouse wants a divorce? If you never keep your word, why do you expect people to depend upon you? If you are manipulative, why do you think people despise you? If you're constantly defensive, why do you think no one shares his opinions with you? If you gossip, why do you think others keep you out of the loop on personal matters?

Sometimes it's not what others do to us but what we do to ourselves that causes us to experience unsatisfying relationships.

Dumb Relationship Choices in Action

We have all said, "I knew better." We get entangled in bad situations because we undervalue sound advice and make rash decisions based on emotions. Doing so forces us to abandon our core values only to taste the bitter waters of disaster.

One man who exemplifies this is Samson. Consecrated to God while still in the womb, Samson was endowed with incredible strength to deliver the Hebrews out of Philistine bondage. God's chosen people had fallen into idolatry. For 40 years, God allowed the Philistines to oppress them. However, He refused to leave them in such a state. So He sent an angel to a man named Manoah and his barren wife to inform them that they would have a son who would be set apart for God until death. God had only a few simple requirements: the boy couldn't drink wine, cut his hair, or go near a dead corpse for a specified time (see Numbers 6:1-8 and Judges 13:5). The parents agreed. Scripture says, "the child grew, and the LORD blessed him. And the Spirit of the LORD began to move upon him" (Judges 13:24-25).

The parents' firm relationship with God was a perfect example for their son Samson to follow. But he didn't. He preferred doing things his way. This was especially true when it came to Philistine women. The

Philistines lived in Canaan, a land inhabited by people God had expressly told the Hebrews not to marry (see Deuteronomy 7:3-4). Samson knew this, yet he *chose* to disobey by insisting upon marrying a beautiful Philistine woman. His parents objected:

> "Isn't there even one woman in our tribe or among all the Israelites you could marry?" they asked. "Why must you go to the pagan Philistines to find a wife?"
>
> But Samson told his father, "Get her for me! She looks good to me" (Judges 14:3 NLT).

With this woman in the picture, Samson was distracted and unable to make a sound decision about marriage. Fortunately, things went south during the weeklong marriage festival, and Samson's efforts to marry this young woman failed.

Samson tried again with another Philistine woman—Delilah. At this point, Samson's supernatural strength had become a thorn in the Philistines' sides. Scripture says Samson single-handedly had killed more than 1000 of their men. Wanting revenge, the Philistine lords dangled 1100 pieces of silver in Delilah's face to entice her to bring Samson down. She took it. Three times she asked Samson to tell her the source of his strength, and three times he lied to her. Feeling mocked, Delilah wept. Her tears were too much; Samson finally told her the truth. Satisfied, Delilah lulled him to sleep, then had a man shave Samson's head. God's Spirit immediately left him.

Now vulnerable, Samson was captured by the Philistines. They gouged out his eyes, threw him in prison, and put him to work grinding grain. Sometime later, during a celebration for the Philistine's pagan god Dagon, Samson stood between two supporting pillars of their temple, called upon God for supernatural strength, and literally brought the house down (see Judges 16:29-30). In the end, God used Samson to defeat the Philistines. But he wasn't around to enjoy the victory. Instead, he perished among a pile of rubble along with 3000 Philistines.

Samson's story reminds me (Ricky) of my friend Reggie, who started a relationship with a questionable woman. Friends and family warned him. He didn't listen. Eventually their relationship, like all of her others, became volatile. She even threatened him, "I am going to put your eyes out." He dismissed her threat. Then after one chilling fight, she poured acid on his eyes while he slept—blinding him for life. I saw him months later as I drove down the street. This once active and strong man now was being taught how to use the guide stick for the blind. It was hard for me to see just how his choices had redefined his life.

Think Through Relationship Choices

Ready to stop the vicious cycle? Want a better, healthier way to conduct a relationship? Bishop T.D. Jakes cautions, "Good decision making in relationships and business results from a process of reflection—discernment—decision."[1] This can be done in the following ways:

1. Reflect on what we have in the relationship—the good, bad, and ugly.
2. Discern if the relationship is worth fighting to keep.
3. If the answer to question number two is yes, decide to keep it by any means necessary.

Albert and Allison learned this lesson while facing the end of their marriage in a cold courtroom in Georgia.

The judge pounded his gavel, "Divorce granted." Allison stood there shocked. After 15 years and five children, this is all she had to show for it? Failure? She sat thinking over the events of the past few years. Their marriage had generated so much distrust and frustration that they could not fathom staying together. Both had allowed friends and associates to bring unhealthy moral and ethical dynamics into their lives. Albert more than Allison seemed to be the most frustrated and tired. He wanted his freedom; she wanted more time with him. Neither one seemed to be able to fill the other's needs. Their constant bickering led them both to bad decisions and eventually to divorce. The reality of her new "marital" status ripped a hole in her heart. Not knowing what else to do, Allison picked up her purse and slowly, sadly left the courtroom.

Albert, however, whistled a tune of freedom as he bounded down the courthouse steps. His lawyer reminded him that for the divorce to be official, he still had to finalize some paperwork and take it back to the judge. Albert called me (Ricky) to give me an update on the proceedings. As his mentor, I was alarmed and asked him to come to my office immediately. We talked and Albert listened. After weighing the impact of his decision, he changed his mind. Albert realized he didn't want the divorce after all. So he called his attorney to halt the proceedings. Albert and Allison stayed married vowing to work things out. With courage and prayer, this relationship was saved.

If you follow the same simple steps that Albert followed, you too can save a valuable relationship:

Seek wise counsel. Before making a major decision, seek counsel from someone you trust. As you *reflect* on your relationship challenges, that person will listen with an objective ear. (We will discuss the importance of wise counsel in more detail in chapter 18.)

Listen with a discerning heart. After sharing your heart, listen to the other person's observations. He or she will speak to you from a place of shared beliefs, core values, and life philosophies. As you're listening, discern if this relationship is worth fighting to salvage. Weigh the pros with the cons. Give it a fair evaluation.

Respond decisively. Once you've listened to the counsel, follow the sound advice. So often when we seek advice, we really just want someone to agree with us. However, for our relationships to last, we must shed the rose-colored glasses and decide if the relationship is worth the fight. If it isn't, walk away. But if it is, put a solid plan into action. That plan may require you to swallow your pride and give more of yourself. You may have to stop controlling the relationship and give the other person room to mature. Finally, you just may have to grow up. Whatever is required, just do it. You'll save not only the relationship, but you'll also save yourself.

Chapter 3

DUMB FINANCIAL AND BUSINESS DECISIONS

"If money be not thy servant, it will be thy master."

Francis Bacon

WHEN JOSEPH JETT, former Wall Street trader at a securities firm, was fired in 1994 and his accounts frozen, people wondered why all his money was in one account. The answer is simple: Smart people can make bad financial decisions.[1] I've made my share. That's why I (Deborah) could hardly wait to see what our survey participants would call their dumbest financial decision ever. Here's a sampling of their responses:

- "Racked up $75,000 in unsecured debt; we pay almost as much in finance charges as we do in tithes. The shame and the guilt are almost unbearable."
- "Bought a friend's business without doing due diligence and analysis first. Disaster."
- "Turned down a promotion because I thought it was happening too soon."
- "Took out a loan to pay off credit cards and then ran the credit cards back up; now my debt has doubled."
- "Quit a job without having already secured another one; I've been unemployed ever since."

- "Did not further my education by taking advantage of the tuition reimbursement benefit offered by my employer."

- "Married my college sweetheart who I knew would not be the best husband for me. In so doing, I relinquished a scholarship to law school and my dreams of becoming a family lawyer."

- "Fell for a Ponzi scheme and lost $30,000 in savings; as a financial professional, I should have known the 30 percent return was too good to be true."

- "Loaned money to a friend knowing she probably would not pay me back. She didn't."

- "Made an impulsive decision to give to a charitable cause and thereby deprived my family of much needed funds."

- "Pursued a career that offered financial gain only; very frustrated and unfilled."

- "Branched out on my own without adequate working capital and financial reserves."

- "Gambled away my limited funds to try to get more."

- "Dropped out of high school in the twelfth grade."

- "Married a man without any knowledge of his credit history."

- "Left a long-term job to pursue another career-track when I had only a few years before full retirement with a lifelong monthly pension of 60 percent of my gross salary."

Heard enough? I cannot close out the list without sharing one of my dumbest financial decisions. Many, many years ago when I was single, fresh out of college, and new to the big city of Los Angeles, a woman from my church came to me and expressed her desire to attend the annual denominational conference held out of state. She was short on funds and simply needed to pay her $100 share of the hotel accommodations. To this day, I cannot figure out why I did not just lend her the $100. Rather, I entrusted my credit card to her, and she agreed to promptly return it to me after the conference. A week or so passed after the event without a word from her. I cornered her after church one Sunday and asked for the card.

"Oh, I love that card," she exclaimed. "I hate to give it back."

She relinquished it. However, when the statement arrived a few weeks later, the charges totaled almost a thousand dollars. Some of the purchases had been made at local retail stores. She confessed that she had even allowed a popular minister to charge several hundreds of dollars. I was flabbergasted. She began to avoid me at church. I was persistent with my phone calls for her to at least make the minimum payments. Ultimately, I took her to small claims court and got a judgment but never recouped the full amount.

When I reflected years later on why I would be so dumb as to give *anybody* carte blanche access to something as important as my credit, I could conclude only one thing: I was trying to gain acceptance. You see, at our church the pastor and leaders disdained formal education and often referred to anyone who had graduated from college as an "educated fool." Unfortunately, in this instance, I had indeed proven to be one. Needless to say, I finally left that church.

There are numerous other personal and business financial behaviors we can classify as dumb. Let's look at a few and see if any of them resonate with you.

Cosigning

When I was growing up, my mom always had a soft spot in her heart for the less fortunate. Whenever she heard about a need, she made every effort to meet it from her limited resources. My dad never had a high-paying job, but he was an excellent money manager and a great provider for our family of nine. In our small town in East Texas, everybody knew each other's business. My mother was particularly concerned that Neighbor X, an alcoholic and the father of six children, shirked his financial responsibility to his family. His wife struggled to provide their necessities. Once, Mom arranged for Mrs. X to purchase clothes for the children at a retailer on her charge account. Mom guaranteed the storeowner that Mrs. X would pay him. Unfortunately, she did not. I remember Mom struggling to pay the bill from her minimum-wage housekeeping job and being petrified that my dad might find out about it (he was fanatical about maintaining excellent credit).

While my mom's decision to help emanated from a heart of love and compassion, it is never a good idea to guarantee someone's debt. The Bible is very clear on the matter.

> It's poor judgment to guarantee another person's debt
> or put up security for a friend.
> (Proverbs 17:18 NLT)

If you cannot make an outright gift or direct loan to a person in need, pray that God will send someone across her path who can assist her.

Failing to Establish Cash Reserves

Some misguided religious souls equate having inadequate savings with living by faith. When Jesus admonished His disciples not to "worry about tomorrow, for tomorrow will worry about itself" (Matthew 6:34 NIV), He was not advocating a *whatever will be, will be* attitude. Jesus knew "a prudent man foresees evil and hides himself; the simple pass on and are punished" (Proverbs 27:12). When the "evil" of unexpected expenses arise, the smart person will have already hidden away the necessary funds to meet the need.

Regrettably, many people barely earn enough to cover their basic expenses. They cannot begin to fathom having any funds to put aside for a rainy day. However, even in the best of economic times, most Americans have proven to be poor savers. Maybe you, like many, have grown weary of the admonitions to save. I'm convinced, however, that you can always live on less. Just consider that approximately 40 percent of the world's six billion people (over two billion) live on less than two dollars per day.

A smart strategy is to begin to save any amount possible (you could set two dollars per day as the minimum) and work toward a goal of saving three to six months of living expenses. *Caution:* Watch your attitude as your reserves grow; guard against putting your faith in your funds. Saving is an act of good stewardship and not a substitute for trusting God.

> Saving is an act of good stewardship and not a substitute for trusting God.

Being Unequally Yoked

The first thing that comes to most of our minds when we hear of being unequally yoked is the marital relationship. However, marriage isn't the only arena where committing to a relationship with one who does not share our values can prove detrimental. Ask King Jehoshaphat. He reigned as a good and wise king of Judah. "And he walked in all the ways of his father Asa. He did not turn aside from them, doing what was right in the eyes of the LORD" (1 Kings 22:43). Then he made a dumb business decision.

> Sometime later King Jehoshaphat of Judah made an alliance with King Ahaziah of Israel, who was very wicked. Together they built a fleet of trading ships at the port of Ezion-ge-ber. Then Eliezer son of Dodavahu from Mareshah prophesied against Jehoshaphat. He said, "Because you have allied yourself with King Ahaziah, the LORD will destroy your work." So the ships met with disaster and never put out to sea (2 Chronicles 20:35-37 NLT).

Imagine Jehoshaphat's frustration and disappointment. This was not a little rowboat project but a very expensive undertaking requiring lots of capital and labor—and it never got off the ground. As a king known for seeking God, there is no mention of Jehoshaphat ever acknowledging Him about this undertaking.

During my career as a financial professional, I've had a few people dangle the proverbial carrot in my face. They promised great financial reward if only I would partner with them in their venture, issue a fraudulent auditor's report as a certified public account, or compromise in other ways that would ensure the profitability of the proposed partnership. Thank God for the counsel of His Word and that of my godly mentors. I believe with all my heart that God will never bless an unholy alliance. It's just dumb to enter into one.

Being Shortsighted

Back in 1981, Universal Studios (my former employer) called up the owners of Mars, Inc. and proposed a deal whereby Universal would feature M&M's in a new film they were producing. In exchange, Mars would help promote the movie. Mars rejected the proposal. Undaunted, Universal took the idea to the Hershey Corporation. They entered into an agreement to use Hershey's fairly new product called Reese's Pieces, which was enjoying only modest sales.

The film was *E.T.: The Extra Terrestrial* directed by Stephen Spielberg. It was one of the highest grossing films in movie history. Reese's Pieces turned out to be a major star in the film when Elliot, the little boy, used the candy to lure E.T. into his house. Hershey's smart marketers capitalized on the exposure and touted Reese's Pieces as E.T.'s favorite candy. Sales went through the roof. "It was the biggest marketing coup in history," says Jack Dowd, the Hershey's executive who approved the movie tie-in. "We got immediate recognition for our product. We would normally have to pay $15 or $20 million bucks for it."[2] The Mars folks are probably still kicking themselves.

But what about you? Have you ever made a shortsighted decision—such as the respondent cited at the beginning of this chapter who said she refused a promotion because she thought it was happening too soon? Often our insecurity and reluctance to rely totally on God causes us to make such a choice.

Surely you can relate to one or more of the financial or business experiences in the litany of dumb choices we have discussed. I'm convinced every bad decision can be traced to an emotion that overrode sound judgment at the time. In Part 2, we will examine ten of these emotions and offer strategies for escaping their clutches.

CHAPTER 4

DUMB HEALTH DECISIONS

*"Don't you realize that your body is the temple of the Holy
Spirit, who lives in you and was given to you by God?
You do not belong to yourself, for God bought you with
a high price. So you must honor God with your body."*

1 CORINTHIANS 6:19-20 (NLT)

PATRICIA IS A VERY SWEET WOMAN. She loves the Lord and is devoted to her family. College educated. Enjoyed skiing. Her future in advertising seemed unlimited. She had broken through to the six-figure salary range. Unfortunately, she also smoked a pack of cigarettes a day. It was her one weakness. She loved the smell of tobacco. It hooked her when she was 18 years old. The allure of the slender cigarette seduced her into believing that smoking was cool. Then in college, she realized it was an acceptable social habit. By the time she was full swing into her career, she discovered smoking was a wonderful stress buster. She'd often say, "A six-figure salary sometimes comes with a six-figure headache." She smoked for almost 30 years, consuming a pack a day for almost 25. It cost her big time. Lung cancer. She doesn't get out much anymore. Her oxygen tank gets in the way. It's now the constant reminder that her choice for dealing with stress was the wrong one.

Being caught up in the cycle of self-sabotage is unfortunately becoming more common. Consider these national statistics:

- "A recent study indicates that by 2015, approximately 75 percent of U.S. adults will be either overweight or obese." Overweight is defined as approximately 10 percent over ideal body weight; obesity is about 30 pounds or more overweight.[1]

- It is estimated that 70 percent of functional disabilities attributed to the aging process may actually result from our own unhealthy decisions and behaviors, such as smoking, obesity, and a sedentary lifestyle.[2]

- "Chronic diseases—such as heart disease, stroke, cancer, diabetes, and arthritis—are among the most common, costly, and preventable of all health problems in the U.S."[3]

- "Recent estimates of the annual cost to the United States in smoking-related healthcare and lost workdays are at least $100 billion a year."[4]

These alarming statistics reveal that far too many people in the U.S. do not value their health. They don't treat it with respect, forgetting that this precious commodity can quickly be taken from us. Life—the one free gift all of us were given—is the one thing many of us slowly destroy every single day because of our poor health choices. If we don't shape up, our lackadaisical attitudes will be the death of us.

I (Ricky) love people. I pastor them. I talk with them. I laugh with them. I mentor them. I marry them. However, as of late, I've been burying too many of them. Most weren't old in age. I'm only 51, and I've been burying people slightly younger, slightly older, but several around my age. Friends. Colleagues. Smart people who just made dumb health choices. I don't mean to make a broad, judgmental indictment for I've made my share of questionable decisions. However, we need to realize we must stop hurting ourselves. Too many good people work hard to achieve success only to end up losing it because of their choices. However, there is a way out—and it's all about making smart health calls.

Unhealthy Choices in Action

According to the Centers for Disease Control and Prevention, lack of physical activity, poor nutrition, tobacco use, and excessive alcohol consumption are the four main behaviors that contribute to early death due to chronic diseases.[5] These are areas where all we have to do is change our habits.

Lack of Physical Exercise

I have heard every known excuse. The truth is, you have two choices: to live a long, healthy, and prosperous life as God intended, or to live a life riddled with chronic ailments. Sometimes you don't know how unhealthy you are until you are tested.

I was in the airport with my family heading for a working vacation that had many stops over the two-week trip. Once at security, I realized there was a mistake on my itinerary. The ticket counter was half a block down the terminal, so I took off running. I didn't think anything of it until I heard my knees ask my back, "What is he doing?" My brain answered, "I think he's running." My arm reached around and grabbed my collar saying, "Mister, we don't do this anymore." My muscles screamed, "Ouch. That hurts. Slow down." Then my lungs gasped for air. I stopped mid-stride. There I was—a hard-working husband, father, and preacher—with no stamina for a half-block sprint. I had forgotten to take care of the horse that carried my workload. That little sprint forced me back into the gym. This was a defining moment that demonstrated just how quickly my health could slip away from me.

Poor Eating Habits

Families enjoy spending time together—often around the table. This would be fine if most people understood that they should eat to live and not live to eat.

Jeremiah was a normal 15-year-old with a big appetite. His family saw that as a great attribute. In fact, his grandparents often said at family gatherings, "Feed that boy. Look, he can sure put it away." They labeled themselves *big-boned* people. No one talked much about weight or health. They worked long hours and loved watching late-night movies. This became a habit for Jeremiah as well.

Soon, he started urinating frequently at school. He was thirsty all the time and seemed to lose energy. Then, for no apparent reason, he started wetting the bed. His parents took him to the family doctor. The diagnosis disturbed them.

"Jeremiah, you have Type II diabetes," the doctor said. "It comes from being overweight. You are 5'1" and weigh 170 pounds. Your sugar level is 450 when it should be 120."

This shook the family. They researched the disease and helped Jeremiah adjust to his new life challenge, which included insulin shots for a brief time to bring his blood sugar under control. They also took a long look at their food habits. After all, Jeremiah didn't plan or cook the family meals. Seeing the warning signs, the family made a drastic change for the better. They went from junk food to healthier options and from no exercise to being active members of their local YMCA. While it was good that the family made the turnaround, it's sad that their child had to first pay the price for the family's poor eating choices.

Smoking and Drinking

These are two legal activities that cause major health damages. Millions of people are negatively affected by smoking. Did you know that there are over 4000 poisons and carcinogens in one cigarette? According to the American Heart Association, "Cigarette smoking is the most important preventable cause of premature death in the United States. It accounts for more than 440,000 of the more than 2.4 million annual deaths."[6]

Smoking leads to chronic issues such as lung problems and is a major cause of heart disease. A recent study shows that the percentage of smokers in the United States has dropped below 20 percent for the first time since the mid-1960s.[7]

Secondhand smoke is equally harmful. It has been linked to low birth weight as well as an increase in the risk of Sudden Infant Death

Syndrome among babies whose mothers smoked during pregnancy. Secondhand smoke also has been named as an underlying culprit in lung cancer, nasal sinus cavity cancer, cervical cancer, bladder cancer, asthma, and heart disease. An estimated 35,000 to 62,000 deaths are caused from heart disease in people who are not current smokers, but who are exposed to ETS (environmental tobacco smoke).[8]

While smoking is definitely a health stealer, drinking carries with it an equal bag of pitfalls.

> Alcohol can affect several parts of the brain, but in general, alcohol contracts brain tissue and depresses the central nervous system. Also, alcohol destroys brain cells and unlike many other types of cells in the body, brain cells do not regenerate. Excessive drinking over a prolonged period of time can cause serious problems with cognition and memory.[9]

We recommend that if you don't drink, don't start. The Scriptures are replete with admonitions to avoid intoxication. We will leave your personal convictions about drinking between you and the Lord. Romans 14 is an excellent passage to read when faced with questionable behavior; its key message is that everyone should be "fully convinced in his own mind" (Romans 14:5) regarding the acceptability of his choices in God's sight.

We often forget that our lives are not our own. We were put on the earth to serve a purpose for the greater good of humanity. The apostle Paul reminded the church at Corinth about this important truth:

> Or do you not know that your body is the temple of the Holy Spirit who is in you, whom you have from God, and you are not your own? For you were bought at a price; therefore glorify God in your body and in your spirit, which are God's (1 Corinthians 6:19-20).

Anytime we choose to abuse our bodies, we put that purpose in jeopardy. Winston Churchill once said, "Healthy citizens are the greatest asset any nation can have."[10] However, after looking at the previous statistics, it seems most of America's assets are at risk.

Healthy Changes for a Better You

When I think about my health, I remember the apostle Paul's warning to the churches of Galatia: "Do not be deceived, God is not mocked; for whatever a man sows, that he will also reap" (Galatians 6:7). This is a stark reminder to me that the state of my health is in direct correlation to what I do daily. This is why I have learned to change the way I view food, exercise, and rest. I believe in living a smart balanced life. All it takes is a little planning, smart thinking, and the complete understanding that how I treat my body today will be what I live with in my later years.

Eat Smart

Generally, a healthy diet consists of the right balance of carbohydrates, fats, protein, vitamins, and minerals. The best way to achieve this is to prepare healthy meals that include a variety of foods from the five main food groups: grains, fruits, vegetables, meat, and dairy. Eat fats, sweets, and oils sparingly. We must learn to view food as fuel. Yes, it should please the senses, but the main purpose of food is to give energy to the body. Think of a car. If you use the wrong type of gas, the car will not run as smoothly, and it may even experience nasty buildup in the tank. It's the same with your body. The right food keeps the body running smoothly. The wrong food clogs your arteries and makes you a prime candidate for heart disease.

> "Those who think they have no time for bodily exercise will sooner or later have to find time for illness."

Exercise Smart

It's generally recommended that we get at least 30 minutes of cardiovascular exercise plus stretching and weight training at least three days a week. Before you offer an excuse for why you can't exercise, know that according to some researchers, the children of Israel walked 25,000 miles during their 40-year wilderness experience. They also estimate that Jesus walked more than 21,000 miles during His life.[11] Jesus could not have carried out His mission if He hadn't been in top physical condition.

Being fit has more benefits than health. It positions us to accomplish our purposes. The apostle Paul recognized this when he wrote to the church in Corinth: "But I discipline my body and bring it into subjection, lest, when I have preached to others, I myself should become disqualified" (1 Corinthians 9:27). We are called to keep our bodies in good condition. Our fleshly desires should not dictate our eating choices. We must control our passions so our bodies will take us the distance to our destiny. We would all be wise to heed the words of famed British politician Edward Stanley: "Those who think they have no time for bodily exercise will sooner or later have to find time for illness."

Rest Smart

Without adequate rest, your body will not be properly refreshed, nor will your brain be able to think clearly. Jesus was a great role model in that, though He worked hard, He routinely carved out time for relaxation: "And when He had sent the multitudes away, He went up on the mountain by Himself to pray. Now when evening came, He was alone there" (Matthew 14:23). His habits of resting and going into seclusion primed Jesus for the demands of His ministry. He understood that communing with God was essential for renewal and refreshing: "Repent ye therefore, and be converted, that your sins may be blotted out, when the times of *refreshing shall come from the presence of the Lord*" (Acts 3:19 KJV, emphasis added).

In the book, *Creation Health Discovery: God's Guide to Health and Healing*, Monica Reed, MD, points out that, according to the National Sleep Foundation, 100 million Americans suffer from a lack of adequate sleep. Dr. Reed, the senior medical officer of the largest admitting hospital in the U.S., adds that: "Rest involves your whole being, not just your body. Your mind and your spirit need to rest, too. With complete and regular rest, you will restore your health and achieve an amazing sense of well-being"[12]

We know that we have touched only the tip of the iceberg in highlighting dumb health choices. Unfortunately, this remains an area most have not chosen to make a top priority. Here are a few of the dumb choices our survey respondents listed:

- "Refusing medical attention after a car accident to avoid being late to work and facing any disciplinary action."
- "Paying a two-year membership at a gym and not going a single time."
- "Becoming sedentary after being extremely active in various sports."

Every single choice we make concerning our health dictates the quality of life we will experience. So whether you have made the dumb choice of consistently working overtime rather than working out, foregoing annual physicals, neglecting to rest, eating artery-clogging foods, or any other behavior that sabotages your health, it's time to pursue optimal health. Make some new, smart choices today. Doing so will affect you and generations to come.

Part 2

TEN EMOTIONS
that DRIVE
DUMB CHOICES

Chapter 5

ARRESTED BY ANGER

*"Anger is that powerful internal force that
blows out the light of reason."*

Ralph Waldo Emerson

MEET DERRICK. He was 26 and a go-getter who had a passion for life. He was quite handsome; a real lady's man. Derrick was great to be around when things were going well. However, when things weren't going so well, watch out. His temper would rage out of control. He was the type of man who hit first and talked later. It was a behavior that had gone unchecked his entire life.

One day while driving with friends in Los Angeles, traffic was unusually heavy. Suddenly, a space opened and Derrick tried to pass. Unfortunately, he slammed into the back of another vehicle. Derrick was clearly wrong and knew it. But that did not stop his anger from rising. The young driver of the stylish Pontiac jumped out of his car in a fury, and the two men exchanged only a few words before their fists took their communication to another level. Derrick's friends tried to restrain him to no avail. Because he was the better fighter, Derrick beat and chased the other man down the street. The young man quickly spotted a shovel lying on the ground at a nearby construction site. Snatching the shovel, he spun around and hit Derrick on the left side of his face and shoulder. Blood gushed from Derrick's face. An emergency call from an onlooker brought the police and an ambulance racing to the scene.

When Derrick came home from the hospital, I (Ricky) was stunned at his appearance. He was wrapped in bandages from his face to his shoulder. His skin never properly healed. To this day a huge gash almost like the imprint of the shovel remains on his face. It is a stark reminder that anger, when mishandled, can leave a lasting impression.

Do you have a memory of when you flew into a rage? Do family and friends tell those around you to duck for cover when your anger starts to escalate? Ready for a change? Let's review a few guidelines on how to express your anger in a healthy way so you can avoid making a dumb choice.

Understanding Anger

Natural and necessary, anger is like the exclamation point in our lives that screams: "We have a problem. Fix it now!" Anger is generally defined as a strong feeling of displeasure because of being wronged. It is triggered by external circumstances as well as our self-talk, which stirs up feelings about things that haven't happened or are based on erroneous information. "Anger signals your body to prepare for a fight. This reaction is commonly classified as 'fight or flight.'"[1] At that moment, we breathe faster, our blood pressure rises, and our hearts race. While this is required in an emergency, remaining this way too long affects our health. Anger is known to cause backaches, insomnia, skin disorders, heart attacks, stroke, high blood pressure, moodiness, and more.

Anger, however, is not a primary emotion; it masks underlying feelings such as frustration, disappointment, fear, sadness, disrespect, rejection, and helplessness,[2] emotions we often have difficulty admitting much less confronting. So we resort to anger. However, anger isn't immediate. It's like the workings of a light switch. Though we see the light instantly when the switch is flipped, the light actually responded to the electricity that flowed through a series of wires to get to the bulb. Anger is the light at the end of our emotional networks. Our "light switch" is an incident. Say for example that while you are trying to make a point in a conversation, you're repeatedly interrupted. Tired of the disrespect, you unequivocally tell the person to stop talking and listen. The primary emotion you felt was disrespect. The anger you expressed was the result of not being respected.

Feeling angry is not wrong. It is a God-given emotion. In the Bible, Jacob's anger was aroused while speaking with his wife Rachel. He was frustrated that she was demanding that he give her children when God was the one who had kept her from being able to conceive (Genesis 30:1-2). Jesus created a whip of cords to drive out the moneychangers selling their wares at the temple. Their actions triggered His anger because God's house was being disrespected: "And He said to those who sold doves, 'Take these things away! Do not make My Father's house a house of merchandise!'" (John 2:16). Both men's responses fit their situations. However, anger becomes problematic when we abuse others or ourselves.

Poor Behavior Choices

How we handle our anger separates the adults from the children. Though Derrick's story was extreme, it's not unique. All you have to do is turn on the TV, read a newspaper, or scan the Internet to see stories of furious politicians, celebrities, and famous sports figures.

One athlete who paid a hefty price for her anger is Serena Williams. She is the younger of the Williams sisters who, at the time of this writing, dominate women's professional tennis. She was penalized a point on match point after screaming and shaking her racket at a line official who called a foot foul. For Williams to show passion on the court isn't unusual. What was unusual was her *choice* to use foul language and threaten the official with bodily harm. The official reported her comments to a higher authority. Warned earlier about her unsportsmanlike conduct, the official penalized Williams a point, which cost her the U.S. Open Championship in 2009. Not only did Williams lose the match, she also was later fined a reported $82,500 and warned that she "could be suspended from future U.S. Opens if she has another 'major offense' at any Grand Slam tournament in the next two years."[3] Because of one dumb choice, Williams's future actions on the court will be thoroughly scrutinized.

Perhaps neither of these stories exemplifies how you express your anger. Maybe you consider yourself even tempered, but you have a habit of bottling your feelings until they explode at the most inopportune time. Perhaps you give people the cold shoulder. Maybe you hold on to grudges or throw tantrums. If you've used any of these behaviors to express your anger, then you, too, have handled your anger irresponsibly. A more responsible way to handle anger is to step back. This allows emotions to cool, minds to clear, and our mouths to stay closed. One person in the Bible who could have used a step back is Moses, a great leader who wrestled with anger his entire life.

Through various circumstances, Moses, a Hebrew, was raised as a grandson of Pharaoh during a time when all Hebrews were enslaved in Egypt (see Exodus 2:1-10). Though Moses was reared as one of great privilege, anger was brewing inside. Perhaps it was because he had watched his people for 40 years labor under slavery. His anger finally erupted as he watched an Egyptian beat a Hebrew. In that instant, Moses snapped. He killed the Egyptian and hid his body in the sand. He assumed that no one had witnessed the murder; however, the next day when he reprimanded two Hebrews for fighting each other, one of them chided him about killing the Egyptian. He knew it would be just a matter of time before Pharaoh would hear about it. Moses fled Egypt and lived as a fugitive for 40 years.

> "Control your temper, for anger labels you a fool" (Ecclesiastes 7:9 NLT).

Healthy Responses to Anger

I believe anger can be healthy when managed properly. When I'm faced with a heated situation, I remind myself of Solomon's wise words, "Control your temper, for anger labels you a fool" (Ecclesiastes 7:9 NLT). This helps me keep a cool head under pressure.

Recently I (Ricky) was rushing through the Atlanta airport with a lot on my mind—mainly the thought of getting home. As I headed to my gate, I walked straight to the counter to address a seat issue. Because I had approached the counter at an angle, I didn't see the roped-off line of people that stood about ten feet away. Immediately, a man berated me as if I had committed a felony. I turned. Realizing my mistake, I quickly moved toward the back of the line. However, his biting comments about my lack of eyesight echoed throughout the waiting area. Though thoroughly embarrassed, I caught myself before I responded in anger. I simply apologized and told him his ranting wasn't necessary. He made a bad decision. I made a good one. As livid as I was, I realized this situation was not a hill to die on. I had to stop, think, weigh the value of the moment, and consider the consequences. Fighting at Gate A28 was not my idea of how to end a wonderful ministry trip where I had touched the lives of thousands.

Steps for a Better Choice

Focusing on the big picture allowed me to make a wise decision. The steps of stop, think, weigh the value of the moment, and consider the consequences aren't new. They are the same principles Jesus applied when He faced an angry mob that had come to arrest Him in the Garden of Gethsemane.

It was the night of the last supper. Jesus and His disciples were leaving the garden where He had just finished praying. The heavily armed soldiers, led by Judas, had come to arrest Jesus:

> Jesus fully realized all that was going to happen to him, so he stepped forward to meet them. "Who are you looking for?" he asked.
> "Jesus the Nazarene," they replied.
> "I AM he," Jesus said. (Judas, who betrayed him, was standing with them.) As Jesus said "I AM he," they all drew back and fell to the ground (John 18:4-6 NLT).

When the soldiers didn't respond, Jesus asked again who they were looking for. They repeated they wanted Jesus. "'I told you that I AM he,' Jesus said. 'And since I am the one you want, let these others go'" (John 18:8 NLT).

Unwilling to let Jesus go without a fight, Peter angrily drew his sword and cut off the ear of the servant of the high priest. Jesus reprimanded Peter, "'No more of this!'" (Luke 22:51 NIV). Then Jesus touched the man's ear and healed him, thus preventing more bloodshed.

This is a clear example of grace under fire. Being the Son of God, Jesus could have easily overpowered the soldiers. However, He kept the bigger picture in mind—protect the disciples and save humanity by dying on the cross. Both objectives were more important than His personal safety. So what did Jesus do? He practiced self-restraint and poignantly talked His way through the moment. By keeping the objectives in the forefront of His mind, Jesus confirmed His earlier statement to His Father: "'While I was with them in the world, I kept them in Your name. Those whom You gave Me I have kept; and none of them is lost except the son of perdition, that the Scripture might be fulfilled'" (John 17:12).

Your Challenge

Anger will come, but don't lose heart. Know that if you follow the above steps, you won't burn your reputation nor torch your future opportunities. Try this practical exercise to help you manage your anger:

1. Determine the real reason you're angry. Write it in a journal. Seeing your thoughts gives you a safe and private place to vent.

2. Share your thoughts with a levelheaded person. Then let him judge whether your anger is valid. People who know you can often help you stay balanced and out of trouble.

3. Give yourself time to cool down. The moment you're offended is not the best time to solve problems. Instead, take a step back. Then later, with a cool head, you're more likely to find a peaceable solution since your emotions are not overpowering your logic.

4. Finally, decide to forgive those who have offended you. Explain how you feel and do it without extreme emotion so that you're heard. Do it in the manner you would want to be approached if you committed the wrongful act.

Prayer

Father, thank You for the mercy that You constantly extend to me when I violate Your boundaries and grieve Your heart with my disobedience. Help me to extend that same grace to others when I would desire to respond in anger to frustrations, hurts, and disappointments. Help me to deal with my anger in a positive and constructive way that glorifies You. I release it now. In the same manner that You have forgiven me, I forgive every person who has trespassed against me in any manner. Thank You, Father, for the peace in knowing I'm doing Your will Your way. In the name of Jesus, I pray. Amen.

Chapter 6

FUELED BY FEAR

"Only when we are no longer afraid do we begin to live."
Dorothy Thompson, American journalist

FEAR BLINDS US. It's an emotion that clouds sound judgment and drives us to make poor choices. We can fear a myriad of things, such as love, success, failure, and change. However, when we let fear dictate our life direction, we limit ourselves to experiencing only those things that do not disturb our sense of comfort. We don't realize that some *scary* things are meant to push us to greater heights.

Secretly, Winnie feared failure. It's what drove her to be a great managing editor. For the last 15 years, she had successfully navigated her family's award-winning small community-based magazine. Her tough-as-nails demeanor had helped the magazine weather many storms; however, the recent economic downturn was different. She cut staff, eliminated departments, and consolidated positions without giving pay increases to remaining staff. When vendors hiked their prices, Winnie passed the increase on to advertisers and consumers. Bad idea. Once-loyal advertisers stopped buying full-page ads. Subscriptions dwindled while newsstand sales plummeted. Her bold moves raised the collective eyebrows of her board of directors. She knew they questioned her decisions, but despite her best efforts, expenses still exceeded revenues. The more she crunched numbers, the more she feared losing it all.

Winnie's tiny editorial staff begged her to create a website. With an online presence, they reasoned, she could regain the quickly declining customer base. Winnie balked. She didn't want to risk spending money on a medium that might not have instant financial rewards. Her advertising staff found possible new vendors online. They were less expensive and claimed to offer the same quality of services. Winnie shunned the idea because she didn't have a personal relationship with them.

Her husband suggested she meet with his friend Ted. He was a marketing genius who might have some fresh ideas on how to retool the magazine. Winnie wouldn't entertain the thought. Exasperated, her husband said, "At least try the website. Who knows? It might work." Winnie refused to listen. Her husband warned her, "Sweetheart, you have to quit being afraid of the unknown. Entertain new ideas. If you don't, you won't have a magazine." His words proved true.

> Anytime fear fuels our decisions, we arrive at the place we were trying to avoid.

When Winnie arrived at work the following day, the chairman of the board was waiting in her office. He handed her an envelope that detailed a fair severance package. "Winnie," he said, "we go back a long way, so this is hard for me. Things aren't working out anymore. We want to go in a different direction. Thank you for your years here."

Hurt beyond belief, Winnie saw her 15-year run at the magazine go down the drain. How had it all come to this?

Fear had dictated Winnie's choices. Anytime fear fuels our decisions, we arrive at the place we were trying to avoid. Winnie feared losing the magazine, and she did.

What have you lost because of fear? Ready to end its grip on your life? Let's explore how this debilitating emotion limits people's choices and learn how to develop wise responses to seemingly fearful situations so you no longer make dumb decisions.

Unhealthy Fear: A Mind-Killer

In the 1984 science-fiction film, *Dune,* the character Paul Atreides says this about fear: "I must not fear. Fear is the mind-killer. Fear is the little-death that brings total obliteration."[1] This quote is a great backdrop for how fear can control our decision-making process, ultimately shackling our lives.

Fear is an intense emotion that causes us to expect something with alarm or apprehension. It puts our minds and bodies on alert. All of our decisions are based on how to protect ourselves from seemingly impending doom or some disadvantage. Dr. Caroline Leaf says there is a direct correlation between fear, how our bodies react to it, and our mental state while in its grip:

> Faith and fear are not just emotions, but spiritual forces with chemical and electrical representations in the body. Consequently, they directly impact bodily function. Every emotion results in an attitude. An attitude is a state of mind that produces a reaction in the body and a resultant behavior.[2]

She believes you can immobilize yourself with worry. This type of fear traps, intimidates, and chases you until you lose the very thing you were trying to protect.

Fear can also trick and frustrate you into believing something that just isn't true. This aspect of fear puts you into stress mode, forcing you to become reactionary. Among the emotions you may encounter are hate, worry, anxiety, anger, and hostility—all fear-based emotions.[3]

Trish and George are an example of this. They had a big fight because George thought he heard his young wife say to someone on the phone, "Don't tell my husband." Thinking the worst, he interrogated Trish the minute she hung up. She tried to gloss over the questions. However, he pressed the issue, and even accused her of being unfaithful. After several minutes of this, Trish exclaimed, "It is impossible to surprise you. I was talking to your mother. We were making plans for your birthday next week, and I did not want her to slip and tell you." Embarrassed, George apologized. (George is ten years older than Trish, and perhaps this age gap has caused him to feel insecure. Nonetheless, fear overrode his common sense.)

Fear can impair our decision-making process. Gregory Berns, director of the Center for Neuropolicy at Emory University in Atlanta, Georgia, further explains:

> Ultimately, no good can come from this type of decision-making. Fear prompts retreat. It is the antipode to progress. Just when we need new ideas most, everyone is seized by fear, trying to prevent losing what we have left.[4]

Dr. Berns suggests that fear muddies the mind and prevents us from discovering any creative solutions. This aspect of fear is demonstrated through the biblical parable of the talents (Matthew 25:14-30). A man traveling to a faraway country distributes his money among three of his servants to manage in his absence. Two servants immediately invest the money, earning a 100 percent return. The third servant hides the money given to him in the ground for fear of losing it. When the master returns, he is quite pleased with the high return the two servants earned, and he gives them more responsibility. However, he scolds the servant who hid the funds in the ground. Not only that, but he takes the money from him and gives it to the servant with the largest amount, saying: "To those who use well what they are given, even more will be given, and they will have an abundance. But from those who do nothing, even what little they have will be taken away" (Matthew 25:29 NLT).

For Winnie, George, and the servant, fear crippled their decision-making skills and limited their view of their options.

Fear Traps in Action

In addition to being unable to discern your options, you can be tricked out of choice opportunities because fear clouds your judgments. This was the case when the nation of Israel, while coming out of slavery in Egypt and heading to the Promised Land, became trapped by fear. They were on their way to what was described as "the land with milk and honey" (Exodus 33:3). This was a land that Abraham, the father of their nation was promised (Genesis 12:1-5). They were just a few days out of Egypt when fear trapped them. They allowed their fear of running out of water and food to drive them to lose sight of the great opportunities to have their own homes and a new life. Moses describes this trap in Numbers 20:2-5:

> There was no water for the people to drink at that place, so they rebelled against Moses and Aaron. The people blamed Moses and said, "If only we had died in the Lord's presence with our brothers! Why have you brought the congregation of the Lord's people into this wilderness to die, along with all our livestock? Why did you make us leave Egypt and bring us here to this terrible place? This land has no grain, no figs, no grapes, no pomegranates, and no water to drink!" (NLT)

They were overwhelmed by the challenges of the moment and the possibilities of failure. Fear robbed them of vision. They could not see beyond their temporary problems. They turned on their leaders who were trying to lead them away from the chains of Egypt to a new beginning. They left Egypt with more than supplies and food (Exodus 12:36); they brought the fear that had grown up in their hearts with them to the Promised Land. Sometimes you can be physically free from a place but not free from its emotional grip. If you are not careful, one challenge or hungry moment can place you under fear's lock and chain once again.

Healthy Responses to Fear

According to nationally certified counselor and life coach Dwight Bain, there are five levels of behavior in dealing with fear:

Level 1: Go numb and do nothing—Fear paralyzes all decision-making skills.

Level 2: Passive pleasing—Avoid conflict by pleasing everyone though inwardly frustrated.

Level 3: Mediocrity in the middle of the road—Refuse to take a definitive stand.

Level 4: Active and assertive expression—Take a stand and get straight to the point with little finesse.

Level 5: Energetic or "Do it all with enthusiasm"—State strong convictions with joy. Act decisively and inspire others around you.[5]

He advises that the most effective routes to making a great decision are using either levels four or five. When someone is active, assertive, and energetic, she feels confident she can overcome her fear. Acting in this manner resembles what the apostle Paul reminds the church at Philippi: "I can do all things through Christ who strengthens me" (Philippians 4:13).

These levels describe how I (Ricky) faced a financial fear as a young husband and father. My family and I enjoyed packing up the van and going to Disney World for vacation. We never stayed at the expensive hotels for fear of overspending. However, the Grand Floridian always intrigued me. It seemed to be the top hotel at the park. I wanted to stay there, but I was always too afraid to consider it a possibility.

One year, my desire and curiosity got the best of me, so I made a quick drive to the hotel; its splendor made me salivate. Swallowing my fear, I looked for a rate card. As I scanned the price list, I noticed that the lowest price for a one-night stay in a double-bed room was $250. Though very expensive for my family of four, I determined to make this happen. I held the picture of the hotel in my mind, and the image prevailed over my fear of being unable to afford the stay. The following year, I set aside enough money for a two-night stay at the grand hotel of my dreams. We checked in early and asked for late checkout. We all packed into one room with one TV, but it was a treat beyond our imagination. A strategic plan to save the money prevented fear from depriving us of a memorable vacation.

Your Challenge

Think about a current situation where fear has stumped you. Evaluate your response in light of the five levels of fear described above.

Prayer

Lord, I refuse to be paralyzed by fear. You have called me to advance and not be passive. Help me not to accept a mediocre existence; but rather, to believe You can do more than I can ask or imagine because of Your power at work within me (Ephesians 3:20). Thank You for standing with me even when I am harshly assertive and have little finesse. By Your grace, I will become energetic and enthusiastic. I will have strong convictions, act decisively, and inspire others around me. In the name of Jesus, I pray. Amen.

CHAPTER 7

GALVANIZED BY GREED

"That man is the richest whose pleasures are the cheapest."

HENRY DAVID THOREAU

DO YOU FREQUENTLY WONDER what it would be like to have greater possessions even though you already have an abundance of things? Do you sometimes refuse to help others financially for fear that doing so will diminish your personal reserves? Do you have a particular possession you cannot imagine giving up? Do you have stuff in every nook and cranny of your home to the point where you are virtually out of space? Have you ever disparaged or disadvantaged someone for personal gain? Are you ready to face your greed?

Greed is that *excessive* desire for more of something than is needed, usually money or possessions. From the Bible to the boardroom, greed has always been at work—and it never shows up alone. It is accompanied by its close relatives Carl Covetous (who strongly desires the possessions of another), Mary Materialistic (whose preoccupation with acquiring things often dims her eyes to noble values and the needs of others), and Danny Deceitful (who engages in all kinds of dishonesty to help Greed achieve its objectives).

In 1 Kings 21, we read the story of King Ahab, who coveted a field adjacent to his estate. It was owned by Naboth, an Israelite who had inherited it from his father and had no desire to sell it—even at the fair price Ahab offered. Refusing to take no for an answer, Ahab's evil wife, Jezebel, bribed a couple of scoundrels to falsely accuse Naboth of blaspheming God and the king. The authorities convicted him and ordered him stoned to death along with his two sons—thus paving the way for the covetous king to obtain the land. Did the king pay a price for his actions? You bet. He died in a battle, and the dogs licked his blood as prophesied by Elijah (1 Kings 21:17-19; 22:37-38). Further, God pronounced judgment on Jezebel. "And concerning Jezebel the LORD also spoke, saying, 'The dogs shall eat Jezebel by the wall of Jezreel'" (1 Kings 21:23). Indeed, the dogs ate her entire body, leaving only her skull, feet, and the palms of her hands (2 Kings 9:30-37).

Now, we readily acknowledge that greed is often at play in high places of our society and in various corporations; however, it has no socioeconomic boundaries. In 2 Kings 5, we encounter a greedy servant. When Naaman, the Syrian general, offered the prophet Elisha money and clothes for curing him of leprosy, Elisha refused to accept them. However, Gehazi, Elisha's servant, could not resist the pull of materialism. He made a dumb choice. He ran after Naaman and his entourage and told them that Elisha had changed his mind and now wanted to accept their gifts. Supposedly, Elisha desired to give them to two young prophets in his training institute who Gehazi claimed had just arrived for a visit.

When Gehazi returned home, he hid the items and reported for duty to his master. Elisha, having discerned his greed and deceitfulness, confronted him about it. Consequence? Elisha pronounced judgment upon him, "'Therefore the leprosy of Naaman shall cling to you and your descendants forever.' And he went out from his presence leprous, as white as snow" (2 Kings 5:27). Gehazi's greed affected not only the quality of his life but also that of his descendants. They would all suffer from the dreaded, socially alienating disease.

The instances of greed in post-biblical times are innumerable. In the 1987 movie *Wall Street*, Michael Douglas played an Oscar-winning role as Gordon Gekko, the ruthless corporate raider who shamelessly and memorably proclaimed "greed, for lack of a better word, is good. Greed is right, greed works." In popular culture, Gekko became and has remained a symbol of unrestrained avarice.

The movie was fictional, but the 2001 Enron Corporation scandal was real. In 2000, the energy company boasted over $100 billion in revenues and employed over 22,000 people. *Fortune* magazine named it "America's Most Innovative Company" for six years in a row. Then in 2001, it was revealed that the company's financial strength and profits were based upon systematic accounting fraud designed to inflate profits and keep its stock prices high. The once celebrated entity became the symbol of corporate corruption. Employees lost their jobs and pensions. In 2006, Enron's former top executives, Kenneth Lay and Jeffrey Skilling, were found guilty of the charges in the corporate scandal that led to

> Sadly, once a person becomes accustomed to certain conveniences and pleasures, he often experiences anxiety about losing them and goes to great lengths to ensure that he will always have them.

the company's demise. Lay died of a heart attack a few weeks after the verdict, and Skilling was sentenced to more than 24 years in prison.[1] Greed had wreaked its havoc.

The average person may feel detached from these stories of greed. However, let's not forget that the greed of lenders, individual borrowers, and investment brokers brought the world's major economies to the brink of destruction in 2009. Unbridled greed also caused investment broker Bernie Madoff to engage in the largest ($50-billion) Ponzi scheme in history in which he defrauded thousands of unsuspecting, but eager-for-high-return individual investors, businesses, charities, and foundations around the world. He is serving a 150-year prison term. At his June 29, 2009 sentencing, he declared, "I live in a tormented state now, knowing of all the pain and suffering that I have created."[2] All decisions borne out of greed will ultimately have their painful consequences.

Root Cause of Greed

King Solomon declared, "Whoever loves money never has money enough; whoever loves wealth is never satisfied with his income" (Ecclesiastes 5:10 NIV). What makes us want more, more, more? First, I believe that one of the root causes of greed is the desire to obtain and maintain as many creature comforts as possible. Sadly, once a person becomes accustomed to certain conveniences and pleasures, he often experiences anxiety about losing them and goes to great lengths to ensure that he will always have them. Second, society highly regards people with wealth; for those who suffer any degree of low self-worth, the pursuit of self-esteem through abundance can become addictive. The fear of loss of such abundance can motivate many evil deeds. Finally, the thought of having to depend on God or others for basic survival can be a scary proposition and a real motivator to pursue abundance. I talked to a wealthy (Christian) businessman recently who was adamant that his days of flying coach class were long gone; the discomfort and inconvenience were simply too much to bear. How soon are we spoiled.

Jesus weighed in on the issue of greed in no uncertain terms. He told a parable about a rich farmer who reaped such an abundant harvest, he had no place to store the excess.

> And He said to them, "Take heed and beware of covetousness, for one's life does not consist in the abundance of the things he possesses."
>
> Then He spoke a parable to them, saying: "The ground of a certain rich man yielded plentifully. And he thought within himself, saying, 'What shall I do, since I have no room to store my crops?' So he said, 'I will do this: I will pull down my barns and build greater, and there I will store all my crops and my goods. And I will say to my soul, "Soul, you have many goods laid up for many years; take your ease;

eat, drink, and be merry.'" But God said to him, 'Fool! This night your soul will be required of you; then whose will those things be which you have provided?'

"So is he who lays up treasure for himself, and is not rich toward God" (Luke 12:15-21).

What have you done with your abundance? Have you simply stored all your cash, real estate holdings, stocks, and other assets for your future benefit? Has greed caused you to pursue that elusive place where you can "take your ease" and never have to worry about experiencing the discomfort or inconvenience of lack? Indeed many people work day and night to acquire enough reserves to allow them to take their ease. Like the prosperous farmer in the parable, they embrace the greed credo: "Get all you can and can all you get."

Greed and Anxiety

As you would expect, there is great anxiety inherent in greed. Such anxiety often fuels evil and dumb choices. Clearly, the farmer's goal was to be able to enjoy life and to ensure that he would never experience lack. Even though he was a farmer and understood the principles of sowing and reaping, his greed blinded him to the truth that he could have sown his excess crops into the lives of the needy and reaped earthly and heavenly rewards. Unfortunately, he did not think beyond his selfishness.

While driving down a busy street recently, I (Deborah) noticed a huge sign on a storage building. It simply read, "Nowhere to put your extra stuff? Store it here. First month's rent only $1." I thought, *Except for unusual temporary circumstances, why store it in a bigger barn? Why not just give it away?*

"Just a little bit more" is how John D. Rockefeller answered the question, "How much money is enough?" Is it possible, you may ask, to reach a point where we are finally satisfied with what we have? Must we always battle this insatiable giant called greed? Indeed, we can keep greed under subjection in our lives but only through the power of the Holy

Spirit. We cannot let our guard down and ever think that the problem has been eliminated once and for all. King Solomon cautioned, "the eyes of man are never satisfied" (Proverbs 27:20). Greed will always compete for first place in our hearts. Once we replace our love for God with our love for goods, the idol is set. "You can be sure that no immoral, impure, or greedy person will inherit the Kingdom of Christ and of God. For a greedy person is an idolater, worshiping the things of this world" (Ephesians 5:5 NLT). It's time to cast down the idol.

The Cure for Greed

Generosity is the opposite of greed. Indeed, it is the most powerful antidote for greed and its infamous relatives. In my effort to be on guard against greed and to resist making idols of my possessions, I have decided to make it a habit to dispossess myself of or give away one item (or more) each time I buy a similar item—whether it's clothing, furniture, books, or whatever.

The other day I purchased a pair of shoes at the mall. When I arrived home, I immediately went to my closet and selected several pairs of practically new shoes that I've been planning to wear when I fully recover from foot surgery. I bagged them up to give to a local charity. I made haste to deliver them the next day because I knew that I could easily talk myself into keeping them. Did God require me to give the shoes away? No. However, I know my tendency to quickly bond with things I really like. Therefore, I'm making every effort to "wear the things of this world as loose garments" as my late mentor, Dr. Juanita Smith, admonished. For me, that means making generosity one of the foundational principles of my life.

I am often reminded of a certain glue that permanently binds items in craft projects and mends broken things. It bonds instantly to whatever it contacts. The label strongly warns that if the glue makes contact with the skin, it can have painful consequences. I've had a few encounters with the glue, and believe me the warning is true. You have to be careful to use it according to the maker's instructions. Likewise, God our Maker has warned us to avoid bonding with our possessions and to use them for His purposes. "You will be made rich in every way so that you can be generous on every occasion, and through us your generosity will result in thanksgiving to God" (2 Corinthians 9:11 NIV).

I have found nothing better for developing faith than ignoring the voice of fear and obeying God in managing the possessions He has entrusted to me. I've encountered the voice of fear many times—especially when God has prompted my husband and me to make a sacrificial financial gift to our church or a special cause. I've often thought, "This gift is going to diminish our cash reserves." Famed missionary Jim Elliot said, "He is no fool who gives what he cannot keep to gain what he cannot lose."

Story has it that in certain parts of Africa and India, a unique strategy is used to catch monkeys. The hunter cuts a hole in a coconut, scoops out the insides, and replaces it with the monkey's favorite food. Attracted by the smell of the food, the monkey sticks his hand into the opening, gets a fistful of goodies, but cannot get his hand out. While he is busy clinging to the food, the hunter captures him. Because the monkey will not let go, he becomes a prisoner of his greed.

Letting go can be a scary proposition for those who have had little or no experience in what it means to walk by faith. In his book, *A Hole in Our Gospel*, Richard Stearns relates the story of how he struggled with God's call for him to give up his cushiony seven-figure salary as president of a luxury china company to become president of World Vision USA. He and his family made the smart choice to obey God and to walk away from their ten-bedroom dream home, luxuries, and conveniences. God has highly exalted him and is using his work to bring him before great men and women on the world stage. I consider Richard a great success because he overcame the gravitational pull of worldly thinking, rejected greed, and did not confuse success with possessions. Further, he refused to measure his worth by his wealth.

Your Challenge

What is the one possession or position that you would have the most difficulty releasing? Your home? Your luxury car? That diamond ring?

The corner office? Why? What value or benefit do you derive from it? Be honest with yourself about this. Remember to stay on guard for ways that your attachment to it may lure you into making a dumb choice. Now, stop and pray the prayer below.

Prayer

Father, You know how much _____ means to me. I confess that I have bonded with it and it has the wrong place in my heart. I know that You want me to wear the things of this world as loose garments. Help me to develop the right attitude toward this possession (or position) and give me the willingness to release it if You require me to do so. In the meantime, show me how I can use it for Your glory now. I want to lay up treasure in heaven and to become rich toward You by serving others with my possessions. In the name of Jesus, I pray. Amen.

CHAPTER 8

INJURED BY IMPATIENCE

"The impatient may not always be wrong on issues, but they are almost always wrong in their attitudes."

ROUSAS JOHN RUSHDOONY, THEOLOGIAN

DO YOU CONSTANTLY CHECK your watch or the clock in your car when stuck in traffic? Do you tap your foot in the midst of a drawn out conversation? Do you hurry your family along if you feel they are a little slow because you are in a rush to get to your destination? If you've exhibited any of these behaviors, you may be wrestling with impatience.

If you are an impatient person, you're often restless or short-tempered, especially when irritated, delayed, or opposed. It also means you live your life in the state of "hurry up" or "now." Waiting is not first on your list, nor is it a trait you wish to acquire. Life is too slow for you, especially when you're going after something big, such as college, a dream job, or marriage.

Being in a constant state of "now" perfectly describes how Clyde once approached his life. Whatever he wanted—money, women, power, and freedom—he had to have it instantly. Driven to be the best, Clyde sought ways to leap ahead of his peers to quickly seize his dreams. He left home at 18, married at 19, worked a full-time job, and went to college at night.

Clyde did everything with fervent passion. However, he never took vacations nor did he take time for himself.

Fast-forward 15 years. Clyde constantly snapped at coworkers. He ignored his wife's pleas to slow down. His relationships began falling apart, and his dreams seemed further from reach. Living life in a rush had depleted Clyde. But he charged ahead anyway. Until one icy night while in a hurry to get to a company banquet, Clyde lost control of his car on a steep curve. It flipped several times before landing in a crushed heap. Days later, he woke up in traction at the hospital. He had injured his spine. In a rush, Clyde had forgotten to buckle up. His wife, who had worn her seatbelt, had walked away from the accident uninjured. He eventually left the hospital, and after months of recovery, learned to walk again. He later shared with me (Ricky) that his time of recovery taught him he had to be patient to heal. "But I just hate waiting," he admitted. "It makes me frustrated. I want to be first. I want to be the best. And I want it now."

Are you like Clyde? Are you allowing impatience to sabotage your future? Do you understand the need to wait, but don't know how to do so constructively? Let's look at a few strategies for eliminating impatience.

The Cost of Impatience

Impatience has a huge price tag; it can cost you your health, your relationships, and your perception of reality.

Impatience Robs You of Total Well-Being

Research published in the *Journal of the American Medical Association* in 2003 found that impatience was a chief factor in health issues. In that study, scientists stated, "Impatience and hostility—two hallmarks of the 'type A' behavior pattern—increase young adults' long-term risk of developing high-blood pressure."[1] A "type A" behavior pattern describes people who are driven, competitive, impatient, and aggressive. High-blood pressure is known to lead to heart disease, kidney disease, and strokes.

In addition to your physical health, impatience also affects your emotional and mental state. Frustration is an outgrowth of impatience. As the frustration mounts, you become angry or depressed at your inability to immediately make your life happen. Bottom line: Impatience can make you sick. Or, as in Clyde's case, send you to the hospital struggling to walk again.

Impatience Destroys Relationships

Impatience can cause you to become short-tempered, irritable, and insensitive toward others.[2] You also may be unable to show compassion. In addition, impatience weakens your decision-making skills, leaving you more susceptible to compromising your core values and beliefs.

Such was the case with Abraham and Sarah. Here was an older, childless couple to whom God, on several occasions, had promised countless descendants (Genesis 12:1-3; 13:14-17; 15:1-6). This was the couple's hope. But as the years passed, their hopes dwindled.

Impatient, Sarah told Abraham to father a child with her maid Hagar, an Egyptian servant. He did, and had a son named Ishmael. However, Ishmael was not the son God promised. Isaac was, and he was not born until 25 years after God first promised the couple descendants. But now there were two sons instead of one. Understanding that the covenant promise belonged to Isaac, Abraham hoped God would bless Ishmael nonetheless. Answering his prayer, God blessed Ishmael and promised to make him into a great nation also (see Genesis 17:20).

Would to God Abraham and Sarah had waited upon His timing. To this day, their impatient decision is felt around the world as modern-day Arabs, who are in constant conflict with the Israelis, claim descent from Ishmael.

Impatience Distorts Your Perception of Reality

Impatience is more than an emotion. It's also a preconceived thought about what your life should look like.[3] Anytime we say we're impatient, we're really saying, "What's going on in my life right now does not look like the vision I have for it." Dissatisfied with life, you do things to push yourself toward where you think you need to be.

That was John, a man driven to raise a family that would never feel the pains of poverty he had as a youngster. He vowed that his family would never be poor or struggle, and they would be educated and have a personal relationship with God. But to achieve his ideal, he insisted that his five children conform to his vision. Because of his domineering parenting style, all of his children rebelled. They became distant. His wife used to tell him, "You are not a very patient man. One day you may lose all you love because of your impatience. People love you, but people need time. You can't just drive and push everybody."

> The secret to overcoming impatience is to embrace every season of your life as a divine appointment.

Now older and with his wife dead, John sits at home alone struggling in the dungeons of regrets and confusion. His children rarely visit. It's as if they all silently voted and agreed: The pain of relating to him is greater than the pain of staying away. Because of his isolation, John has a new sense of reality. He now believes he did something wrong. But it took losing everything he held dear to reach that place.

A Season for Everything

The secret to overcoming impatience is to embrace every season of your life as a divine appointment. I like to describe those seasons in farming terms: sowing, waiting, and reaping.

Sowing

Even before going out to the field, a farmer knows what he wants to plant. He preps the soil by tilling the ground and nurturing it with fertilizer. Then he plants the best seed he can find. In your "sowing" season, invest in your future: Go back to school. Hit the gym. Hire tutors for your children. Save money to pay for the initial big investment. This is the most expensive season in our lives because it contains no immediate reward.

Waiting

After planting, a farmer waits for the crop by occasionally watering his field, dusting it for bugs, and hoping the weather is favorable. For you, waiting means you have spent, invested, studied, graduated, and done all you can to reach your goal. Now, you nurture your skills by reading books or subscribing to magazines about your field of expertise. You go to seminars and conferences to gather new ideas. Waiting is a critical season because it keeps you prepared to harvest your crop at a moment's notice. You never know when God will say "now" to your dreams. It's similar to the advice Paul wrote to Timothy: "Preach the word! Be ready in season and out of season" (2 Timothy 4:2).

Reaping

When the crop is ready, the farmer goes out—along with his hired hands—to bring it in. Reaping a crop takes work, but it's exciting. If the weather was favorable, the crop usually provides a greater return than what the farmer planted. Reaping your harvest is called payday. It's when your investment affords you a comfortable retirement. Your education affords you a remarkable career. Your patience allows you to enjoy a strong marriage, wonderful family, and fabulous friends. The longer your waiting season, the bigger the reward and the more you will appreciate the harvest and sowing seasons. Bottom line: Don't rush your seasons. Experience each one with a joyful spirit and reap greater rewards.

Patience's Reward

When we learn to value each season, we put our hearts and minds to the task without becoming impatient. Jennifer Hudson and Kellie Pickler are great examples of this principle. Both were on the hit TV show *American Idol*—a national competition to find the next "singing sensation." Both young women lost. However, because they continued to cultivate their skills in their waiting season, they eventually achieved a foothold to their dreams. Hudson snagged the role of Effie in the movie *Dreamgirls* in 2006 and won an Oscar for Best Supporting Actress for her performance. Pickler recorded her first CD, *Small Town*

Girl, which debuted number one on *Billboard*'s top country charts in 2006. Not bad for women who learned to wait patiently despite the disappointment and temporary roadblocks to their dreams.

Your Challenge

Sowing. Waiting. Reaping. Which season are you currently experiencing? How's your patience level? Use this exercise to help you see a clearer picture of where you stand:

Write your feelings about your current season and how you believe you are faring in it.

If you need help, consult a wise friend. Then write three things you can do to improve your response to your season.

Check your impatience levels. We normally can't pinpoint our own impatience. So ask a few trusted friends the following questions:

1. Would you consider me a patient or impatient person?
2. When was the last time you saw me in an impatient state?
3. How do I behave during my times of impatience?
4. Have you ever been affected by my impatience?

Use the responses to the questions above as a prayer tool. Try the prayer below for starters.

Prayer

Lord, I now realize I have a tendency to be impatient. It is not something I always recognize. You said they that wait upon the Lord shall renew their strength. I trust You to renew my strength during my times of impatience. I will run through this temptation and not be weary. I will walk and not faint. Bless those around me who may have been affected by my impatience and may they now be inspired to grow as they see me change and become more patient. In the name of Jesus, I pray. Amen.

Chapter 9

SACKED BY STRESS

*"Stress is a state we experience when the demands that
are put upon us cannot be counter-balanced
by our ability to deal with them."*

RICHARD LAZARUS, PSYCHOLOGY PROFESSOR

IT'S GOING TO BE A GREAT DAY, Donna thought. She had gotten off
to a good start—rising early to pray, meditating on an awesome passage
of Scripture, dressing to go exercise. Then the phone rang and things
started to go downhill. She learned that her mother's adult day care center would be closing permanently within 48 hours. Because of a break-
down in communication, their 30-day notice had fallen through the
cracks. Her mother could not be left alone, so time was of the essence to
find another facility. Donna had an extremely important project due to a
client. She had planned to work on it nonstop for the next three days.

She immediately abandoned her exercise plans and started her search
for a new center. She knew she'd have to make at least one site visit, complete endless forms, and remain on hold on the phone for an eternity for
government and medical office personnel to process the information
required by the new facility. During the stress of it all, with the phone
glued to her head for several hours, she found herself eating cake batter,
processed turkey (parading as a health food despite its extremely high

salt content), and other junk food—plus foregoing the eight glasses of water she vowed to drink as part of her New Year's resolution. Taking the time to cut up all those raw veggies she'd purchased earlier in the week was out of the question.

She not only sabotaged her eating plan, but continued to make other dumb decisions—like showing extreme impatience with well-meaning people whose phone calls disrupted her already tight schedule. She even got into a silly argument with her usually wonderful husband when he arrived home from work. It took two hours of "effective confrontation" for them to get back into harmony.

"Tomorrow will be a new day," Donna said with a sigh. Indeed, it would be, but the impact of some of the day's poor choices would have a lingering effect. Okay, I'm Donna. I (Deborah) sheepishly admit this lest you have read my book, *30 Days to Taming Your Stress*. I promise you, I make every effort to practice what I preach. That day was just one of those off-the-chart crazy days.

Stress and Poor Choices

Stress does that. It can drive you to make bad choices—the chief of which is the failure to just stop, regroup, and restrategize. I can almost sympathize with King Saul for the time he became so stressed he offered a sacrifice that only a priest was authorized to make (1 Samuel 13). To put his dilemma in perspective, imagine this scenario: You are the head of a military group on a special government assignment ordered by the president of the United States. Your mission is to conquer a strong and well-equipped army in a certain country. The president has a special military envoy who has the code to a secret weapon that would assure victory. In fact, you actually have the weapon in your possession. The envoy is currently on assignment in another country, but has agreed to come to your location to input the code within seven days after you and your troops arrive.

In the meantime, the enemy mobilizes for battle. They outnumber your troops more than 20 to 1. When your group sees such an overwhelming opponent, they panic and start to hide or run away. You are caught in a dilemma because you *know* how to input the code to the weapon; however, the United States strictly forbids anyone other than a special envoy from performing this act. You could be court-martialed for violating the law. What would you do as Day-7 comes to a close and the envoy is nowhere to be found? Do you input the code or wait for him?

This was the kind of dilemma King Saul faced. The Israelites were in a military conflict with the Philistines. Samuel the priest had promised the king that he would come to the battlefield in seven days and offer a burnt offering to the Lord on their behalf. God had always been Israel's secret weapon no matter how powerful the enemy. The Philistine army quickly swelled to 30,000 chariots, 6,000 horsemen, and innumerable foot soldiers. King Saul's 2,000 troops hid in caves; some scattered. The pressure was too much to bear. Saul intruded into the priest's office and sacrificed a burnt offering (1 Samuel 13:5-12). He felt he had to make supplication to God; after all, they needed a miracle *now,* and God was the key to their victory.

Dumb choice. The minute he performed the forbidden, priest-only function, Samuel showed up. Saul attempted to justify his action, but Samuel wouldn't hear it.

> And Samuel said to Saul, "You have done foolishly. You have not kept the commandment of the LORD your God, which He commanded you. For now the LORD would have established your kingdom over Israel forever. But now your kingdom shall not continue" (1 Samuel 13:13-14a).

God would not tolerate the king's disobedience—even though he had acted under stress. His action cost him his kingdom.

Now, it's easy for us armchair quarterbacks, with the benefit of 20-20 hindsight, to say that he should have just exercised more patience and waited. Indeed, he *should* have. But would you have had the faith to wait? The ability to exercise this kind of patience and trust comes from having an intimate relationship with the Father.

What a contrast Saul's response was to that of King Jehoshaphat, who reigned later in Israel's history, when he heard that three armies were mobilizing against him. Though he feared, he was quick to pray, to affirm his faith in the Divine Deliverer: "For we have no power against this great multitude that is coming against us; nor do we know what to do, but our eyes are upon You" (2 Chronicles 20:12).

Moses also demonstrated such faith when he stretched forth his staff and commanded 600,000 men plus women and children to step into the Red Sea with the Egyptian army breathing down their backs. God showed Himself strong and parted the waters. The Israelites crossed over on dry land while the entire Egyptian army drowned (Exodus 14).

Even Moses, however, though he knew God intimately and knew the importance of obedience, got sacked by stress. He made a dumb choice when the pressure mounted in the wilderness. The multitude found themselves without any drinking water—for the *second* time during their trek to the Promised Land. On the first occasion, in a place called Horeb, God had instructed Moses to *strike* a certain rock (see Exodus 17:6). Moses obeyed and water gushed forth in abundance and everybody was satisfied. However, on the second occasion, in the desert of Zin, God gave Moses and his brother Aaron a simple command: Call the people together and "*speak to the rock* before their eyes, and it will yield its water" (Numbers 20:8, emphasis added). Still grieving over the recent death of their beloved sister Miriam (Numbers 20:1) and frustrated at the endless complaints of the multitude, Moses made a dumb decision under the pressure of it all that kept him and Aaron out of the Promised Land.

> And Moses and Aaron gathered the assembly together before the rock; and he said to them, "Hear now, you rebels! Must we bring water for you out of this rock?" Then Moses lifted his hand and *struck the rock twice* with his rod; and water came out abundantly, and the congregation and their animals drank.
>
> Then the LORD spoke to Moses and Aaron, "Because you did not believe Me, to hallow Me in the eyes of the children of Israel, therefore you shall not bring this assembly into the land which I have given them" (Numbers 20:10-12, emphasis added).

My heart aches for Moses as I read this story. He had spent almost four decades trying to lead this ungrateful bunch to freedom. Now, because of a single decision made at the height of frustration, he was not going to see his dream fulfilled. The pressure had impaired his judgment. Notwithstanding, the message is clear: God will not tolerate disobedience—whatever the justification.

> During a stressful period, it is best to stop and make the stress itself the most important issue to be addressed.

Have you ever made a bad decision under stress? Perhaps you spoke a harsh word, resorted to a dishonest or violent act, or some other God-dishonoring behavior.

Coping with Stress

I believe that each of us would be wise to develop a preestablished coping philosophy for how we will or will not behave when stress rears its head. We must first recognize its symptoms and not be in denial about them. Such symptoms may include: increased heart rate, overeating, excessive irritability with others, inability to stay focused on a task, becoming emotional over small irritations, decreased sex drive, headaches, and many others. During a stressful period, it is best to stop and make the stress itself the most important issue to be addressed.

For example, when I feel my adrenaline starting to go into high gear, I immediately begin taking long, deep breaths. I know from extensive research that this slows down my heart rate and helps me to stay in control of my emotions. Sometimes, I'll take a 5-10 minute nap so that my fatigue doesn't impair my judgment. Finally, one strategy that always works for me is to go into a room, turn the lights off (or put on eyeshades), lift both hands high into the air, and surrender to God in total darkness. Many times, I will pray: *Father, I'm coming to You in total darkness because I need You to shine Your light on this situation. I know that according to Daniel 2:22, You reveal deep and secret things, You know what is in the darkness, and the light dwells with You. Please show me what to do now.*

These are just a few of the ways I put into practice Psalms 46:10: "Be still, and know that I am God." It is critical to become still and focused long enough to know that the God of the universe is never without a solution to life's problems. When I get still and stop rushing to find an answer, God will often bring the answer to me. I've experienced this many times when facing tough decisions.

Oh, that we would learn to keep a divine perspective on every problem, especially since our perception of a problem determines the level of our stress. Author Catherine Pulsifer explains, "How we perceive a situation and how we react to it is the basis of our stress. If you focus on the negative in any situation, you can expect high stress levels. However, if you try and see the good in the situation, your stress levels will greatly diminish."

Your Challenge

Make every effort to minimize this deadly emotion. Pray, exercise, delegate, sleep, laugh, forgive, do right—do everything you can to walk in the tranquility of His presence. Try the prayer below (and meditation on the related Scriptures) for keeping the pressures in your life in perspective.

Prayer

Father, I believe that all things are working together for my good because I love You and I am called according to Your purpose (Romans 8:28). You are the faithful God of the universe and nothing is too hard for You (Jeremiah 32:27). I rejoice in knowing that Your thoughts toward me are thoughts of peace and not of evil, to give me a future and a hope (Jeremiah 29:11). Therefore, I will be anxious for nothing (Philippians 4:6). I cast all my cares upon You for You care for me (1 Peter 5:7). In the name of Jesus, I pray. Amen.

CHAPTER 10

CAUGHT BY CURIOSITY

*"Curiosity, in spite of its many charms, can
bring with it serious regrets."*

CHARLES PERRAULT, AUTHOR OF *BLUEBEARD*

I (DEBORAH) GREW UP IN an environment where inquisitiveness was discouraged. My parents and elders deemed it disrespectful if a child asked "Why?" about any assertion adults made. When children are rebuked too often about this, it can wear them down and silence their yearning for learning. Fortunately, I had a passion for reading, and it opened up a world of information. Besides, my schoolteachers were wise enough to allow free expression and discovery.

Someone once said, "Curiosity is the knocker at the door of wisdom." Inquisitive behavior is natural to all humans. Babies, for example, are curious about everything. It is amusing to watch them touch or attempt to taste everything around them. This curiosity continues into adulthood. Because of it, people have made marvelous discoveries and inventions that have improved the quality of life for all. If you can fathom it, consider what your life would be like if some smart, curious person or group had never discovered, developed, or invented the wheel, electricity, anesthesia, the printing press, the telephone, the microwave oven, and—my favorites—the computer and the Internet.

Curiosity That Killed the Cat

Not all curiosity is good nor results in a positive outcome. In the French fairy tale *Bluebeard,* a young woman is forced through an arranged marriage to become the wife of a rich nobleman who sports a despicable blue beard. One day he leaves on a long trip and gives her permission to explore the castle and to amuse herself with all the fine jewels he has kept locked away. He gives her the key to every room in the house, but reminds her not to enter the one that he has always forbidden anyone to access. Her curiosity gets the best of her, and she disobeys his order. Inside, she finds the bodies of all his former wives hanging from the walls. Their curiosity had spelled their doom.

She is horrified. She makes every effort to eliminate any evidence that she had entered the room. However, when Bluebeard returns, he sees the indelible bloodstains on the room key. Furious at her disobedience, he attempts to murder her also. Fortunately, her brothers break into the castle just in time and kill him. As his only heir, she inherits his entire estate. She gives much needed financial assistance to her family and uses part of the money to marry a worthy man who makes her forget all about her miseries with Bluebeard.

There are numerous other stories of curiosity killing the cat. Of course, the most well-known, and the one with the most far-reaching result, is the story of Eve, the first woman on earth—and it's no fairy tale. Her curiosity caused her to taste the God-forbidden fruit of the Tree of Knowledge of Good and Evil. Results: the fall of mankind.

In myth, legend, or reality, those who gave in to their curiosity often suffered dire consequences. Many times when one is curious about the wrong thing, it can affect the rest of her life and that of others.

Such was the story of Dinah, the beautiful daughter of the Jewish patriarch Jacob and his wife Leah. When her family settled in Canaan, she was surrounded by a world very different from the ways of the Israelites. One day, she "went out to see the daughters of the land" (Genesis 34:1). Perhaps she was curious to know how the young ladies lived, dressed, and generally fared in such a worldly culture. In any event, she made herself vulnerable to lustful men and other pitfalls. It took no time for curiosity to kill this cat.

> And when Shechem the son of Hamor the Hivite, prince of the country, saw her, he took her and lay with her, and violated her. His soul was strongly attracted to Dinah the daughter of Jacob, and he loved the young woman and spoke kindly to the young woman. So Shechem spoke to his father Hamor, saying, "Get me this young woman as a wife" (Genesis 34:2-4).

When Dinah's brothers heard the young prince had defiled their sister, they (especially Simeon and Levi) were livid. The fact that Shechem wanted to marry her did not assuage the brothers' anger; it laid the foundation for their revenge. Though the Israelites were under strict orders from God not to intermarry with the people of Canaan, Dinah's brothers pretended to embrace the idea—on one condition. All the men of Shechem had to be circumcised (as was required of all Jewish males). They all consented to the requirement. On the third day after the circumcision (Genesis 34:25), while the men were still very sore and less able to defend themselves, Simeon and Levi went into the city, slew the prince, his father, and all the other males there. Dinah's curiosity resulted in her losing her virginity and innocent men losing their lives.

Like Dinah, Carol (not her real name) grew up in a sheltered environment. Immediately after high school, she joined the U.S. army. Her primary goal was to distance herself from her conservative Christian parents and their church-going lifestyle. She wanted to explore the world. However, within 18 months her curiosity about the world of drugs and her desire to fit in overrode her judgment. She found herself kicked out of the military for underage drinking and drug use. Her humiliation accelerated her downward spiral. When I interviewed her for this book, she explained her journey:

> After I was kicked out of the army as well as sentenced to jail for a short term, I was too embarrassed to return home

to the West Coast, so I stayed in Texas—and continued my alcohol and drug abuse. Calls to my parents became fewer and farther in between. Soon I stopped calling them altogether. I missed them terribly, but the shame I felt was too great. I knew I was a disappointment.

A few years later, I returned to my home state and made brief contact with them. They were elated and relieved to see me, but it was short-lived. I soon disappeared again.

> It is inherent in human nature to want to experiment; however, it's also in our nature as smart people to avoid things that are obviously bad for us.

Shortly thereafter, I became pregnant. During a party weekend in the local mountains, I gave birth to a beautiful, premature baby boy—right there in the cabin…no doctors…no nurse…only the crude assistance of a friend who had the wherewithal to call an ambulance. My baby tested positive for drugs. The local children's protective services agency took him away and placed him in a foster home. They demanded that I go into a drug rehabilitation program if I had plans of raising him myself.

When I saw the helplessness of this beautiful child and realized his total dependence on me, my heart melted. The weight of my parental responsibility hit me like a ton of bricks. I knew I had to make some changes. I spent almost two years in a residential rehab center. I also reconnected with God and my wonderful family, who welcomed me back with open arms. I'm on my way now. I'm determined to be the best possible mother for my son.

Carol's journey, born out of curiosity, had caused many years of heartache and pain for those in her circle of love. She's no longer pursuing unhealthy curiosities; she now knows all too well their pitfalls.

Curiosities to Avoid

It is inherent in human nature to want to experiment; however, it's also in our nature as smart people to avoid things that are obviously bad for us. Perhaps the bad things are not always so obvious; therefore, at the risk of being redundant, here are at least four areas where you would be smart *not* to indulge your curiosity.

Drugs

Many people, young and old, have experimented with drugs for no other reason than to find out what it feels like to be under their influence, to discover what pleasure awaits. Before they know it, they are snared in a lifetime of addiction and suffer many financial, relational, and other losses. I have a close relative who battled drug addiction for over 30 years. He, like Carol, had tried it the first time in the U.S. military. My family and friends offered many prayers and made intercession for him. Finally, God arrested his heart, and now he is evangelizing his former drug friends.

Doing drugs is dishonoring to the body. God is holding each of us accountable for our physical well-being. "Or do you not know that your body is the temple of the Holy Spirit who is in you, whom you have from God, and you are not your own? For you were bought at a price; therefore glorify God in your body and in your spirit, which are God's" (1 Corinthians 6:19-20).

The Occult

Our desire to know the future can lead to big trouble. It all starts out innocently. "What does my horoscope say today?" Soon, you may find yourself calling a psychic hotline to get a heads-up on a relationship: "Is Mary the woman I'm to marry?" "Is my husband having an affair?" Numerous passages in the Bible warn against involvement with astrology, divination, witchcraft, sorcery, and other occult practices. The prophet Isaiah advised: "Someone may say to you, 'Let's ask the mediums and those who consult the spirits of the dead. With their whisperings and mutterings, they will tell us what to do.' But shouldn't people ask God for guidance? Should the living seek guidance from the dead?" (Isaiah 8:19 NLT).

The Private Matters of Family and Friends

Your prying into the affairs of others will surely earn you a place on their "Do Not Trust" list if they were to find out. Will access to certain confidential information really improve the quality of your life? Why do you want to know such things anyway? Maybe it's time to get a life. Most importantly, know that the Bible puts such behavior in the same list as *murder* and *stealing* of offenses Christians should never be guilty of: "If you suffer, however, it must not be for murder, stealing, making trouble, or prying into other people's affairs" (1 Peter 4:15 NLT).

Employer's Confidential Records

Let's assume the new payroll clerk inadvertently left a copy of your company's payroll register on the copy machine. You discover it and decide to make a personal copy to peruse later. This could lead only to trouble. What would be your objective in doing this? To gossip to another person about it? You run the risk of becoming demoralized if you discover a huge disparity between your compensation and that of others you deem to be less qualified. Your best bet would be to find the payroll clerk and return the report immediately.

This is just a brief list of curiosities to avoid. I'm sure you could add several more based upon your experiences.

With the computer revolution, the Internet has become a library without walls where we can indulge our passion for knowledge on any subject. Because of His love and concern for His creation, God will continue to give people insight and wisdom to improve our lives. I believe the best inventions and discoveries are yet to come. We would do well to follow the advice of famed physicist Albert Einstein, "The important thing is not to stop questioning...never lose a holy curiosity."

Your Challenge

When you decide to be curious about something, determine first what God's Word says about it. Then ask yourself these two key questions: *What is my objective in attempting to satisfy my curiosity? Will I have to violate a biblical command or principle to do so?*

Prayer

Father, I pray that You will give me a healthy curiosity about things that will benefit humankind or help me with my personal development. Help me to mind my own business and to resist inquisitiveness about the private affairs of others. Take away all desire to experiment with any substance that is illegal or that will impair my ability to make sound judgments. I want to bring glory to Your name in everything I do and say. In the name of Jesus, I pray. Amen.

Chapter 11

LURED BY LUST

*"But each one is tempted when he is carried
away and enticed by his own lust."*

James 1:14 nasb

WHEN DOLLY SUGGESTED to her husband John that they watch an adult movie together in the privacy of their home, her only objective was to invigorate their stale sex life. Little did she understand that when men—or women—expose themselves to pornographic images, they unwittingly open the door for a lustful spirit to invade their hearts.

Several months later, on a late-night raid to the refrigerator, Dolly caught John viewing a pornographic site on the Internet. She was hurt and bewildered. For John, it was a relief to be "caught in the act." He longed to be free of the pull of the enticing photos, the stimulating sexual language, and the empty pleasure of his frequent masturbation. The guilt was also starting to cause some sleepless nights. Because he held a prominent position in their church and community and wanted to maintain his squeaky-clean image, he had waged his battle for deliverance in isolation.

Dolly felt betrayed. She also felt guilty for planting the seed that led to his cyber-adultery. She demanded that he get counseling. John is now on his way to recovery but is still trying to muster the courage to share his story with other men to help them avoid the subtle trap that almost led to the death of his 25-year marriage. Lust had reaped its reward. James, the brother of Jesus, summed it up this way: "Then when lust hath conceived, it bringeth forth sin: and sin, when it is finished, bringeth forth death" (James 1:15 KJV).

The Nature of Lust

Lust is an intense desire to gratify the senses—be it lust for power, money, or sex. In this chapter, we will concentrate on sexual lust since it is the most common type. The tentacles of lust have reached into high places in the world of sports, entertainment, politics, and religion. It has tarnished the public images and ruined the personal relationships of esteemed celebrities and leaders. Lust will cause you to make some of the dumbest choices imaginable. Because of lust, many have hired the wrong employee, married the wrong person, frequented the worst places, and jeopardized prized business and personal relationships.

In our sex-crazed society, each day brings a constant barrage of lust-inducing images. They are inescapable; they beckon from billboards, movie and television screens, magazine covers, and other media. If that were not enough, it seems that dress codes have been abandoned in every profession as women in the workplace now sport attire more common to "ladies of the night"—showing cleavage and overly exposing other parts of their bodies. More alarming is the fact that godly men can forget about finding relief from the onslaught when attending church. A significant number of church-going women have embraced the world's standard of dress and thus provide continued temptation for men to lust.

The Consequences of Lust

The Bible is replete with stories of lust and its consequences. Let's examine a couple of them.

Amnon, King David's firstborn, waged a losing battle against his lust. He craved to have sex with his beautiful half-sister Tamar (2 Samuel 13). He made a dumb decision to take the advice of his crafty first cousin who told him to feign illness and request Tamar to come to his home to prepare him some food. Once alone, Amnon coaxed her into his bedroom and raped her—finally satisfying his lust, which he had initially labeled as *love*. He immediately felt repulsed by her. Despite her protests, he ordered his servants to throw her out of his house. King David heard about the incident but did not attempt to redress the wrong—within the law as the king or within the family as the father. David's son Absalom was furious that his half-brother had defiled his sister and so callously ruined her future. She could no longer dream of having her own family; she was spoiled merchandise. Absalom loved his sister dearly and plotted revenge for two years. Finally, he had Amnon killed at a special feast he had carefully planned for that purpose. Lust had reaped its final reward.

Of course, we could say "like father, like son" for King David's own lust overrode sound judgment the first time he saw the beautiful Bathsheba:

> Then it happened one evening that David arose from his bed and walked on the roof of the king's house. And from the roof he saw a woman bathing, and the woman was very beautiful to behold. So David sent and inquired about the woman. And someone said, "Is this not Bathsheba, the daughter of Eliam, the wife of Uriah the Hittite?" Then David sent messengers, and took her; and she came to him, and he lay with her (2 Samuel 11:2-4a).

Talk about cutting to the chase. He simply *saw* her and immediately made the dumb choice to *sleep* with her.

Her husband Uriah was away at war at the time. Later, when she discovered and informed the king she was pregnant, David ordered the army captain to put Uriah on the frontline of battle without backup. He was killed. David married Bathsheba but the baby died. Thus a loyal soldier and an innocent baby died because of actions born out of lust.

It seems that a lustful spirit became a stronghold in David's family. In addition to Amnon's rape of his sister, David's son Solomon, though renowned for his wisdom, was dumb enough to have 700 official wives and 300 concubines who turned his heart away from God (1 Kings 11:3). Solomon's son Rehoboam had 18 wives and 60 concubines (2 Chronicles 11:21).

I (Deborah) pray that the men who read these accounts will take note of the generational impact of the dumb choices these men made and make every effort to resist succumbing to lust.

> The lustful person focuses on pleasing himself—the antithesis of the Christian life which is about *selflessness.*

Of course, women are also susceptible to lust. Take the story of Mrs. Potiphar. Her husband, an Egyptian captain, hired Joseph the Hebrew captive to run his household. However, Mrs. Potiphar was captivated by Joseph's physical appearance and could not control her lust: "Now Joseph was handsome in form and appearance. And it came to pass after these things that his master's wife cast longing eyes on Joseph, and she said, 'Lie with me'" (Genesis 39:6-7).

When he rejected her advances, she accused him of rape. Her husband threw Joseph in jail. Through a series of God-orchestrated events, he was eventually released and promoted to prime minister of Egypt. God always rewards a stand for holiness.

Conquering Lust

Lust is a choice—a motivated choice. A selfish choice. The lustful person focuses on pleasing himself—the antithesis of the Christian life which is about *selflessness.* Lust doesn't stop to evaluate the other person's character or how its actions will impact others. The Bible offers four surefire strategies for victory over this giant.

Resist

Job is most renowned for his steadfastness to God during his extreme suffering at the hands of Satan; however, he should be equally celebrated for his strategy for keeping lust out of his life. He was a wealthy and powerful man. A man in such a position has unlimited access to women. Wealth and power represent security—one of the most critical needs of a woman. Yet, Job was proactive in guarding his sexual integrity. "I made a covenant with my eyes not to look with lust at a young woman" (Job 31:1 NLT).

Herein is an essential key to victory over lust: Cut it off at the pass. In every example that we explored above, the lust of the eyes put the ball in motion. What turns a *glance* at an eye-catching woman into lust is the amount of time invested in the act. One godly man counseled, "If you can discipline yourself not to take that second look, you're home free."

Retired NBA star A.C. Green Jr. proved that a man does not have to succumb to lust. *Sports Illustrated* magazine tells the story of how he began and ended his career as a bachelor and a virgin—and the challenges he faced.

> During Green's rookie season, 1985-86, several Lakers started a pool to see who could make the kid compromise his principles. "It got up to about $600," says teammate Michael Cooper. One player even sent, as Cooper recalls, "one of the best-looking women you will ever see" to Green's hotel room during one road trip. "We really thought we got him," says Cooper. "But he came downstairs the next morning with a big smile on his face and told us he was going to have to start quoting the Bible to us. We gave him grief, but it was all good-natured. We had a lot of respect for his decision."[1]

Despite the various basketball records he holds, most people still remember A.C. primarily for his stance against premarital sex. Now married, he continues to preach celibacy, informing kids about sexual abstinence through the A.C. Green Youth Foundation in Rolling Hills, California. He asserts in media interviews, "I want kids to see that there is more to life than chasing skirts."

Run

Never overestimate the strength of your moral steadfastness when dealing with lust. You may not have as much power as you think you have. "Therefore let him who thinks he stands take heed lest he fall" (1 Corinthians 10:12). You are never more likely to yield to a temptation than when you have put confidence in your ability to resist it. When you have unwisely allowed your glance to turn into a stare and found a receptive target for your lust, or when your unmet needs make you susceptible to someone else's advances, there's only one thing to do: Run. Run for your life.

Mrs. Potiphar was unrelenting in her advances toward Joseph. One day, she "caught him by his garment, saying, 'Lie with me.' But he left his garment in her hand, and fled and ran outside" (Genesis 39:12). This courageous and godly act kept Joseph from sinning against God, his master Potiphar, and his own body:

> Flee sexual immorality. Every sin that a man does is outside the body, but he who commits sexual immorality sins against his own body. Or do you not know that your body is the temple of the Holy Spirit who is in you, whom you have from God, and you are not your own? For you were bought at a price; therefore *glorify* God in your *body* and in your *spirit,* which are God's (1 Corinthians 6:18-20, emphasis added).

Rely

"Walk in the Spirit, and you shall not fulfill the lust of the flesh" (Galatians 5:16). This is a *command,* not a suggestion—and it is the only way not to yield to the strong passions of the flesh. You will need more than a New Year's resolution or a strong resolve. To "walk in the Spirit" is to surrender your longings and cravings to God and to allow His Holy Spirit to lead you each step of the way to victory. That means calling and relying on God during those crucial times when you are burning with a passion that screams to be satisfied. It also means exercising godly wisdom in avoiding environments and situations that can lead to fulfilling those desires.

> Can you build a fire in your lap
>   and not burn your pants?
> Can you walk barefoot on hot coals
>   and not get blisters?
> It's the same when you have sex with your neighbor's wife:
>   Touch her and you'll pay for it. No excuses.
>   (Proverbs 6:27-29 MSG)

Yes, you will pay for it, and only God knows what the price will be.

If you are losing the battle with lust, know that fasting is a good spiritual discipline for bringing fleshly passions into subjection to the Holy Spirit. If you are new to the concept of abstaining from food for spiritual victories, then start on a small scale. Rather than a "water-only" fast, you might consider giving up sweets, your favorite treats, or meat for a few days or weeks. Start wherever you are in your stage of spiritual development. God will honor any effort to crucify the desires of the flesh. Most importantly, keep your goal in mind each time you are tempted.

Replace

I often recall how my high school physics instructor used to hammer home that "no two forms of matter can occupy the same space at the same time." As we rid ourselves of lustful thoughts, we must be quick to replace that void with spiritual thoughts that reinforce our commitment to sexual integrity. Such a transformation of thinking is impossible without a constant diet of the Word of God. "And do not be conformed to this world, but be transformed by the renewing of your mind, that you may prove what is that good and acceptable and perfect will of God" (Romans 12:2). In addition to the Word, we must make every effort to replace old habits that provoked lustful thoughts (steamy novels, sex-starved friends, R-rated movies). No need to make a big announcement about your new strategy; just do it.

From the examples we have discussed, it is clear that lust is primarily stimulated by physical appearance; therefore, I make a special appeal to every woman to be sensitive to the impact you have on men. Use wisdom in selecting your attire. Search your heart to discern your motive for dressing in a way designed to make a man take a second look or to fantasize about how it would be to have sex with you. Do you really want to inspire men to notice you in a way that dishonors your heavenly Father? You may find that dressing more modestly will garner you more respect and credibility with men and women on and off the job.

Beyond Physical Attraction

It is beyond the scope of this book to explore the deeper psychological issues that may motivate lust. Notwithstanding, my friend, Dr. Elvin Ezekiel, who speaks extensively on this matter, had this to say during a recent conversation:

> Some lust is driven by more than the attraction of "eye candy" for the flesh. Some lust is rooted in the emotional or psychological makeup of a person. This is so because of how some people were raised. Some predispositions such as overeating, rage, alcoholism, sexual addictions, and love addictions can also drive the sexual behaviors you find resident in people with low self-esteem. These individuals who struggle with lust cannot just say no. They must first deal with their core issues.

In their book, *Love Is a Choice,* Robert Hemfelt, Frank Minirth, and Paul Meier argue that people with empty love tanks tend to over romanticize or idolize relationships and can become prone to sexual activity. They do this to connect and feel a part of a relationship. They are often unaware of why they do what they do. This then speaks to a deeper problem. A different approach to becoming healthy and operating within proper and appropriate sexual boundaries is needed.

If you are caught in the grips of lust, don't despair. Seek out a qualified counselor who specializes in this area—while putting your faith in the Great Physician to set you free.

Be encouraged by the lyrics to Horatio Palmer's 1868 hymn, *Yield Not to Temptation.* They provide great encouragement for men and women to resist the pitfalls of any sin:

> Yield not to temptation, for yielding is sin;
> Each vict'ry will help you some other to win;
> Fight manfully onward, dark passions subdue;
> Look ever to Jesus, He'll carry you through.

Your Challenge

Make every effort to avoid environmental "lust triggers"; make that covenant with your eyes to focus on other worthy pursuits instead. The more you resist, the stronger you will get. Take your need for attention, for intimacy, or for love to the throne of God. He will supply all your need. He is your Shepherd, and He will not leave you lacking in strength to overcome any obstacle.

Prayer

Father, thank You for the Holy Spirit whom You have sent to help me live a holy life (Galatians 5:16). I want to glorify You in everything I think, say, and do. Help me not to make provisions to fulfill the lusts of my flesh (Romans 13:14). Help me to resist enticing television programs, movies, and sexually explicit materials, and to refrain from lingering gazes at the opposite sex. Teach me to cast down every vain imagination and fantasy, every thought that is contrary to Your will (1 Corinthians 10:5). I know that as I consistently submit to You, I will be able to resist the devil and he will flee from me (James 4:7). I know that apart from You I can do nothing (John 15:5). Therefore, I ask that You give me a strong desire to daily connect with You through prayer and meditation on Your Word. In the name of Jesus, I pray. Amen.

CHAPTER 12

PROMPTED BY PRIDE

*"A man's pride will bring him low, but the
humble in spirit will retain honor."*

PROVERBS 29:23

PICTURE THIS SCENARIO. God empowers ordinary man to achieve an extraordinary result. Man gets accolades and "press" for the accomplishment. Man believes the press and takes full credit for the outcome. Man's independent attitude angers God. God topples man from his throne of self-exaltation. Man is destroyed or learns his lesson and begins a new life of humility. This is the scenario of the rise and fall of pride—it hasn't changed since the beginning of time.

Consider the case of King Herod Agrippa. He persecuted the early church and had James, one of the twelve apostles, put to death (Acts 12:1). He would have executed Peter had the church not prevailed in prayer for God to deliver him out of Herod Agrippa's hands (Acts 12:3-18). He was pride personified.

One day he made a great speech to a group of citizens whose country he supplied with food. He had been angry with them previously, but they had ingratiated themselves with one of his aides and made peace with him. The politically smart group was overly enthusiastic about King Herod's speech, enough to erase the ill feelings of any ego-maniac. "And the people kept shouting, 'The voice of a god and not of a man.' Then immediately an angel of the Lord struck him, because he did not give glory to God. And he was eaten by worms and died" (Acts 12:22-23). King Herod's over-inflated ego caused him to make the dumb choice of accepting the glory that belonged solely to God. Perhaps he was not aware of God's admonition spoken through Isaiah, "I will not give My glory to another" (Isaiah 48:11).

King Nebuchadnezzar was another leader who learned the hard way that "pride goes before destruction, and a haughty spirit before a fall" (Proverbs 16:18). He too tried to take God's glory. He wielded great power. "Whomever he wished, he executed; whomever he wished, he kept alive; whomever he wished, he set up; and whomever he wished, he put down" (Daniel 5:19). One day, as he strolled the breathtaking grounds of his Babylonian palace, he became overwhelmed with pride for all he had accomplished.

> The king spoke, saying, "Is not this great Babylon, that I have built for a royal dwelling by my mighty power and for the honor of my majesty?"
> While the word was still in the king's mouth, a voice fell from heaven: "King Nebuchadnezzar, to you it is spoken: the kingdom has departed from you" (Daniel 4:30-31).

God immediately banished the proud king to a life with the beasts of the fields. His fine grooming was a luxury no longer afforded him. His hair grew like the feathers of an eagle and his nails like the claws of a bird. Rather than the gourmet meals he was accustomed to, he ate grass like the oxen. He even lost his mind. His season of humiliation must have seemed like an eternity, but he had to endure it until he realized "that the Most High rules in the kingdom of men, and gives it to whomever He chooses" (Daniel 4:32). After seven years, God had finished renovating his heart.

And at the end of the time I, Nebuchadnezzar, lifted my

eyes to heaven, and my understanding returned to me; and I blessed the Most High and praised and honored Him who lives forever…

At the same time my reason returned to me, and for the glory of my kingdom, my honor and splendor returned to me. My counselors and nobles resorted to me, I was restored to my kingdom, and excellent majesty was added to me. Now I, Nebuchadnezzar, praise and extol and honor the King of heaven, all of whose works are truth, and His ways justice. And those who walk in pride He is able to put down (Daniel 4:34,36-37).

Surely, the nation suffered during his absence. Indeed, many nations suffer because of the outsized egos of their leaders. For example, after a deadly 8.0 earthquake hit Sichuan, China, in 2008, it was heartbreaking to hear media reports of Chinese officials dragging their feet in accepting water, food, shelter, and medical attention from the United States and other countries while the victims suffered. Asserting self-sufficiency in the midst of such devastation was just plain dumb.

> Pride is an arrogant, haughty estimation of one's importance.

Corporations also suffer from the effects of pride and inflated egos. In his book *Egonomics,* Steven Smith states,

> It is essential in business that we ask ourselves with each decision and action, "By making this choice, am I feeding my ego or attempting to fill my bank account?"…Having and allowing an inner circle of confidants, a mentor, or select leaders (specialists) within your organization the right to speak freely is critical. They must be permitted to offer opinion, feedback, perspective, and even criticism without repercussion. You must be open and willing to suspend judgment, consider their advice, and, if it is the right thing to do, change your direction…The bigger your leadership

role becomes, the greater the likelihood that your pride and ego can become factors. Always remember who you are and where you came from. Chances are, you didn't make it on your own, and you can never afford to think that you can stay there on your own either.[1]

The Perils of Pride

Pride is an arrogant, haughty estimation of one's importance. When we dissect the concept of pride, we can see why God finds it so detestable. Pride is always competing for that place of superiority. Let's see how it looks in action and how it drives us to make dumb choices.

Pride blinds us to our weaknesses and shortcomings. Some people think that if they are excelling in a certain discipline (even in exercising spiritual gifts), then all other behavior is insignificant. If a particular corporate executive's efforts have a positive effect on the bottom line, he may believe it's okay to be insensitive to his subordinates and not to improve his people skills. If the church's membership has quadrupled under Pastor Joe's leadership, he may resent the elder board questioning items on his expense report.

Pride blinds us to the source of our strength and abilities. Here is where it rubs God the wrong way: man's attempt to claim for himself the *glory* (admiration, honor, or credit) that belongs to God. It is ridiculous to be proud about *anything* when *everything* we have comes from God.

Consider the following illustration. Your boss and his wife are coming to your house for dinner tonight. Just as you were preparing to dash to the market for some last-minute items, your neighbor rings the doorbell. She hands you a container, and you immediately recognize her popular gourmet dessert. It is a proven crowd pleaser. You are ecstatic. You serve it that evening, and everybody raves about how delicious it is. Now, how ridiculous would you be if you took the credit for it when all you did was serve it on your best china?

This is what happens when we present our talents, gifts, resources, knowledge, or other accomplishments to the world. We are simply presenting what God has *given* to us. "For who makes you differ from another? And what do you have that you did not receive? Now if you did indeed receive it, why do you boast as if you had not received it?" (1 Corinthians 4:7). I (Deborah) have literally framed this passage lest I forget and start to believe that anything I've done is the result of my hard work and ingenuity. I never want to be guilty of "stealing God's glory."

Pride: The Behaviors and Choices

The questions below are designed to help you come face-to-face with behaviors and choices that emanate from a spirit of pride. Don't rush through the list. Rather, try to think of instances where you have engaged in the particular conduct.

- When facing a tough decision, are you more inclined to analyze the facts before you pray for God's guidance?

- Do you compare yourself with others and rejoice when you have the edge or some clear advantage over them?

- Does it irritate you for people to disagree with you?

- Do you have a "you're not qualified to criticize or correct me" attitude?

- Do you become offended when people don't give you the recognition, respect, or honor you think you deserve?

- Are you frequently appalled by what you perceive as other people's stupidity or limited knowledge?

- Do you think you usually know what's best for those in your circles of interaction?

- Do you find it difficult to admit your mistakes or to apologize even if you are clearly at fault?

- Are you more likely to correct or criticize someone than to compliment him?

- Do you offend people often?

- When someone offends you, do you mentally place him on your blacklist?

- Are you generally inflexible and closed to input on alternate ways of doing things in your personal or business life?

- In conversations with others, are you interested only in the things that concern or affect you?

- When you pray, do you tend to justify your transgressions versus being emotionally broken for hurting God?

An affirmative answer to *any* of the questions above is evidence that pride may be gaining a foothold in your life. You can see how each of your responses will reveal a potential for an unwise choice. It's time to get off the fast track to a fall.

How to Be Humble

"God resists the proud, but gives grace to the humble" (James 4:6). Humbling yourself is surely the most effective strategy for healing when you've made a dumb choice and allowed pride to damage a relationship. I recently confronted a family member about her ingratitude and her attitude of entitlement to my resources. Now, while I do not regret what I said, I do regret the timing. It was her birthday. I initially justified my action by saying I wanted her to know why I wasn't sending a gift. Had I pondered my decision a little longer, I would have realized that no one wants to hear criticism on her birthday. I apologized to her for my poor timing, but I had already done relational damage.

Someone once said, "Swallowing your pride seldom leads to indigestion." Stop and consider now whether you need to swallow your pride and apologize for an unkind or unwise word or deed. It's time to walk in humility.

If you are quick to assert that you are a humble person, watch out. You may be proud about that. Humility is not self-negation or the denial of your God-given strengths and abilities. It is simply a realization and an acknowledgement that God is the source of everything you bring to the table. To walk in humility is to completely embrace the truth of John 15:5: "I am the vine, you are the branches. He who abides in Me, and I in him, bears much fruit; *for without Me you can do nothing"* (emphasis added). We must get this truth into the deepest recesses of our mind. It has changed my life and given me supreme confidence. It will do the same for you.

Learning to walk in humility requires an awareness of our "pride propensities" (see pride quiz above). Since we all tend to be blind to or tolerant of our negative behaviors, we might want to enlist the help of a spiritually mature friend or our spouse to help us stay on a high alert for evidence of them. For example, one of my close friends would often forget to say "please" to restaurant servers—not a wise decision since they handle your food. I got in the habit of completing her request when she would address a server. When she would say, "Bring me some more water," I'd quietly say, "please," which she would immediately repeat to the server. She has improved significantly.

Know that pride will be your greatest enemy to intimacy with God. He refuses to be up close and personal with a proud person. He "resists the proud, but gives grace to the humble" (James 4:6).

Your Challenge

Of what personal skill, talent, or accomplishment are you most proud? Why? How do you feel inside when others compliment you for it? How do you respond to the compliment? List one action you will take in the next few days to reduce pride (review aforementioned checklist for ideas).

Prayer

Father, help me never to forget that apart from You, I can do absolutely nothing. Forgive me for those times that I have taken credit for any accomplishment that You empowered me to achieve. Cause me to continually humble myself so that I may have a close, intimate relationship with You, for You resist the proud but give grace to the humble. In the name of Jesus, I pray. Amen.

CHAPTER 13

INFLUENCED BY INSECURITY

"She perceives that her merchandise is good…"
PROVERBS 31:18

RICHARD DREADED THE FIRST DAY of the month. Lately, it seemed to come sooner than usual. He looked at the stack of bills on his table—staring at him, defying logic: the adjustable mortgage statement reflecting the recently increased payment; the remittance coupon for the loan on his fancy sports car (it was almost as much as the mortgage); the credit card bill for the many Christmas presents he had purchased for family and friends—it would take at least a year to pay off the balance at such exorbitant rates. Yes, he would be able to make the required payments—but just barely.

Richard was a college-educated professional, an up-and-coming executive at a major corporation. *How did I let myself get to the point where I live so close to the edge?* he wondered. Though he asked the question, he wasn't ready to face the real answer—that one overriding emotion that drove his unwise decision to enter all these transactions.

He had bought the house because it was impressive. He often replayed in his mind the *oohs* and *ahs* of everyone who visited him and admired its many amenities. The house gave the impression that he had it all together. And, of course, living in such a posh neighborhood required a car that matched the status of the house. When he attended various social functions, he felt great satisfaction in stepping from the crowd and strolling to the car when the valet delivered it. It made him feel that he belonged.

The Christmas presents? Surely, you don't expect someone who can afford such a fancy house and car to be stingy at Christmas time. His generous gifts made him a favorite with the family. They had great expectations of him as the only relative with a college degree.

Richard was short, walked with a slight limp from childhood polio—and single. Most women didn't consider him especially attractive, but he knew many would be lured by his stuff. Even though Richard had sacrificed his financial stability to perfect his image, he was still plagued with that one emotion that's like the elephant in the room that nobody wants to acknowledge. It's called *insecurity*—and it can drive you to make some really dumb choices.

Insecurity caused Helen to secretly follow her fiancé whenever he canceled a date. She was suspicious of his every interaction with any reasonably attractive woman. Inwardly, she felt she didn't really have what it took to keep him interested in her. If only she had known that such jealousy would surely drive him away. Had she, by the grace of God, embraced Psalm 16:5 (NLT), her response would have been different:

> LORD, you alone are my inheritance, my cup of blessing.
>   You guard all that is mine.

Insecurity is prevalent throughout the Bible. It was insecurity that kept the church leader Diotrephes from allowing visiting leaders or evangelists to speak at his church. The apostle John explained,

> I wrote to the church, but Diotrephes, *who loves to have the preeminence among them,* does not receive us. Therefore, if I come, I will call to mind his deeds which he does, prating against us with malicious words. And not content with that, he himself does not receive the brethren, and forbids

those who wish to, putting them out of the church (3 John 9-10, emphasis added).

Diotrephes could not risk losing the attention, affection, and admiration he enjoyed. His scarcity mentality caused him to believe that something as intangible as feelings were in limited supply. This is a sad commentary for a man or woman of God.

Insecurity Indicators

Most people deny their insecurities and allow them to wreak havoc in their lives. If you are ready to face your uncertainties and inadequacies, review the list of behaviors below. They are strong indicators that insecurity may have a stronghold in your life. Be honest and check the ones you currently exhibit.

1. Defensive/overly sensitive to criticism (view feedback as rejection or a confirmation of inferiority)
2. Extremely jealous (fear that you will be displaced)
3. Materialistic/obsessed with trappings such as fancy cars, designer fashions
4. Intimidating (use anger to manipulate the choices of others)
5. Overly accommodating to others (in an effort to gain approval or acceptance)
6. Highly competitive (even with children or weaker opponents); get esteem from winning
7. Feel inferior due to certain unchangeable physical features
8. View another's *success* (especially that of close friends or family members) as your *failure*
9. Boastful; "toot your own horn" (overcompensating for self-doubt)
10. Play down achievements or deflect compliments (to avoid being envied or rejected)

11. Wear overly suggestive/sexual attire (primarily women); believe it's the only way to get noticed, having defined yourself by your physical appearance

12. Verbally and/or physically abusive (primarily men) in an attempt to gain control

13. Territorial (protective of position or status in an organization)

14. Performance driven; derive personal worth from accolades and achievements

15. Feel unworthy to interact with people who are more beautiful, educated, wealthy, or of higher social standing

16. Name-drop (seek validation and admiration by association with influential people)

17. Hesitant to express a different opinion on a matter (going along to get along; afraid to risk alienation)

18. Make suggestions or ask questions in a tentative, unassertive manner in meetings with others

19. Reluctant to express personal boundaries and preferences in relationships

20. Refuse to undertake challenging work or other assignments (believe failure is fatal rather than a learning experience)

Dumb Choices Born Out of Insecurity

The types of dumb choices that can come from such a list of behaviors are endless. We've already seen an example of bad financial choices with our friend Richard, the smart executive with all the trappings. Insecurity is no respecter of persons; it attacks everybody—at every social, political, and spiritual level.

King Saul is a vivid illustration of this truth. At first glance, there is no apparent reason why he should have been insecure—especially in his position as Israel's very first king. Unlike most of today's leaders, he was divinely *selected*, not *elected* by a fickle majority. Second, he was tall and handsome: "and when he stood among the people, he was taller than any of the people from his shoulders upward. And Samuel said to all the people, 'Do you see him whom the LORD has chosen, that there is no one like him among all the people?'" (1 Samuel 10:23-24). He was unique in a positive way. Let's face it. It increases the average person's confidence to know that his appearance is pleasing to others. Finally, Saul had a strong support system, compliments of God Himself: "And Saul also went home to Gibeah; and valiant men went with him, whose hearts God had touched" (1 Samuel 10:26).

How then, did this leader become so insecure that he spent years pursuing—with an intent to destroy—David, his son-in-law and slayer of Goliath, the giant who had once defied the entire Israelite army?

There are many teachable moments in this saga that spans 15 chapters of Scripture (1 Samuel 17-31), but let me (Deborah) rush to reveal the core issue that plagued Saul. We saw in chapter 9 that he disobeyed God by offering an unauthorized sacrifice. God gave him his termination notice and advised him that He had already found his replacement (1 Samuel 13:14). However, God did not indicate what day would be the king's last day on the job. How confident would you be in your job position if you faced such a reality?

A few chapters later (1 Samuel 17), David comes on the scene and kills Goliath. Ironically, the prophet Samuel had already *privately* anointed David as the new king prior to his encounter with Goliath. "Then Samuel took the horn of oil and anointed him in the midst of his brothers; and *the Spirit of the LORD came upon David from that day forward*...But the Spirit of the LORD *departed from Saul*" (1 Samuel 16:13-14, emphasis added). Although David had been anointed king-elect, it would be quite some time and many stressful days and nights before he would step into the position. God's employment procedures were a little different from modern standards. He fires Saul, but lets him stay on the job; then He hires David but doesn't give him a start date.

But back to the story...The people are thrilled at Goliath's defeat. They go wild with praise for David.

So the women sang as they danced, and said:
"Saul has slain his thousands,
And David his ten thousands."
Then Saul was very angry, and the saying displeased him;
and he said, "They have ascribed to David ten thousands,
and to me they have ascribed only thousands. Now what
more can he have but the kingdom?" So Saul eyed David
from that day forward (1 Samuel 18:7-9).

Knowing that his days as king were numbered due to his prior disobedience, Saul's insecurity goes into high gear, causing him to make three dumb choices:

- He made numerous attempts to slay David even though David had done nothing to incur his wrath (1 Samuel 18–28).
- He once hurled a javelin at his son Jonathan to kill him for supporting David and covering for him (1 Samuel 20:23).
- He had his servant murder 85 priests in cold blood because someone saw one priest conversing with David when he was fleeing Saul's wrath (1 Samuel 22:18).

Yes, the plague of insecurity is still one of the most worrisome problems of even the most accomplished and successful people. What are we to do?

Conquering Insecurity

So far, you may have noticed that this chapter is not about how to build *self-confidence*. I believe self-confidence is a carnal or worldly concept that is dishonoring to God. Scripture declares, "He who trusts in himself is a fool, but he who walks in wisdom is kept safe" (Proverbs 28:26 NIV). The very quest to enhance the sufficiency of the "self" keeps one in a state of fear and uncertainty.

Self is a hard taskmaster. No matter how much you learn, how many cosmetic surgeries you have, or how much impressive stuff you acquire, you will from time to time feel your inadequacy. The stark truth is that we are indeed inadequate—apart from God. Once we settle this in our hearts, we can embrace a new paradigm: *supreme confidence.*

It's no coincidence that David was so confident in asserting that he could conquer the giant; the Spirit of God was upon him. It also follows why Saul was so fearful; the Spirit of God had departed from him. Herein is the essence of supreme confidence. Jesus reemphasized this truth when He declared, "I am the vine, you are the branches. He who abides in Me, and I in him, bears much fruit; for without Me you can do nothing" (John 15:5).

> The very quest to enhance the sufficiency of the "self" keeps one in a state of fear and uncertainty.

This powerful promise has revolutionized my life. The mandate is simple; we must make staying connected to the *vine* our primary objective—fearing and acknowledging our omnipotent (all-powerful), omniscient (all-knowing), and omnipresent (always present everywhere) heavenly Father. "In the fear of the LORD there is strong confidence" (Proverbs 14:26).

No More Dumb Choices

Your personal assessment of your worth will affect every decision you make. Once you start to walk in supreme confidence, here are a few of the dumb choices you will surely choose to let go:

- *Controlling others.* You decide to give others the freedom to make their own choices. Further, you stop fearing that they will make decisions that will disadvantage you.

- *Tolerating an abusive relationship.* You stop believing that the abuser is your last hope for a partner or that you do not deserve better.

- *Dressing overly seductive.* You no longer tie your self-worth solely to your physical appearance. You're a complete person with ideas, opinions, and dignity.

- *Engaging in self put-downs.* You acknowledge your shortcomings and refuse to define yourself by a single one of them. You now value what you bring to the table. You become like the Proverbs 31 woman: "She perceives that her merchandise is good" (Proverbs 31:18).

Your Challenge

1. Note at least two behaviors from the insecurity list that you identified with.

_____

_____

2. Indicate one dumb choice that you have decided to eliminate now:

_____

3. Meditate on Proverbs 8:14 (NLT) for reinforcement of your decision:

> Common sense and success belong to me.
> Insight and strength are mine.

Prayer

Father, I stand on Your Word that assures me that You are able to make all of Your grace abound toward me so that I always have all sufficiency in all things and abound in every good work (2 Corinthians 9:8). I cast down every thought of inadequacy and every imagination that rises up against what Your Word says about who I am and what I can do (2 Corinthians 10:5). I will not allow insecurity to dictate any of my decisions. By Your power, I will walk in Supreme confidence knowing that You make my future secure (Psalm 16:5) and that no one can thwart Your purpose for my life (Isaiah 14:27). In the name of Jesus, I pray. Amen.

CHAPTER 14

GOADED BY GUILT

*"When sins have been forgiven, there is no
need to offer any more sacrifices."*

HEBREWS 10:18 NLT

WHEN RUBY WAS 19, someone murdered her mother, Lola, as she was on her way home from a social work assignment in a shady neighborhood. Lola had taken the bus there because she was temporarily between cars, though she planned to buy a car that very week.

Ruby owned a car but had not offered to give her mother a ride to the high-crime area. After Lola's death, Ruby's thoughts of condemnation were unrelenting. *If only I'd taken her to work...If only I'd been the model, career-oriented daughter she wanted me to be...* Lola was a real go-getter and had expressed concern about Ruby's "low ambition."

Ruby was overwhelmed with guilt. To medicate her pain, she turned to drugs. For over 15 years, she battled cocaine addiction. She abandoned her children—all five born out of wedlock—to relatives and friends. She went to prison. She finally hit rock bottom. That's when she found God.

Today, at age 37, she is a great single parent. She has received numerous community service awards for her work as an anti-drug activist and counselor. When one of her children, still scarred from the abandonment, lashed out at her recently about the pain of growing up without a mother, Ruby calmly explained that she had worked through and overcome the guilt associated with her behavior. She refuses to let her past imprison her. Her resolve has become a broken record: "I'm not going to allow anybody to make me relive my past," she says.

She knows beyond a shadow of a doubt that God has forgiven her for *all* her sins. The blood Jesus Christ shed for her was the only required sacrifice, and it was sufficient. She does not have to sacrifice her present, her peace, nor her potential on the altar of guilt. For "when sins have been forgiven, there is no need to offer any more sacrifices" (Hebrews 10:18 NLT). What a liberating truth.

Dumb Choices Born Out of Guilt

Guilt is a self-inflicted emotional wound that can lead to all types of wrong or unwise choices. Here are just a few examples of the types of decisions that can emanate from guilt.

- Danetta suffers from guilt for working excessive overtime and not spending enough time with her 11-year old daughter, Jessica. She makes the dumb decision to compensate for it by imposing few restrictions on Jessica's social activities and her spending. The child is disrespectful to her mother and resents her for being what she describes as "the worst parent ever."

- Carl remains burdened with condemnation because his wife, Barbara, suffered a stroke many years ago after she learned of his dumb choice to have an affair with her best friend. She never fully recovered. Now he tries to make amends by saying yes to her every demand—which has often landed them in financial hot water and disadvantaged them in numerous other ways. She is faithful in keeping the guilt trip working to her advantage.

- Donna is so determined not to have any regrets when her elderly father dies that she overextends herself and caters to his many unreasonable demands. She doesn't get ample rest, foregoes regular vacations with her husband, and often cancels her plans to attend important events of other family members. "I want to be able to say I did all I could for him," she rationalizes. The very thought of experiencing any remorse in the future has driven her to make a dumb decision: to allow her life to spiral out of balance and to jeopardize the quality of her other key relationships.

- Judas could not overcome his guilt over betraying Jesus. He pleaded with the priests and elders to take back the 30 pieces of silver they had paid him: "'I have sinned by betraying innocent blood.' And they said, 'What is that to us? You see to it!'" (Matthew 27:3-4). His guilt drove him to make the dumbest choice anyone could ever make: "Then he threw down the pieces of silver in the temple and departed, and went and hanged himself" (v. 5). It is important at this point to reiterate our definition of *dumb:* "lacking sound judgment and forethought in light of the circumstances and possible consequences." Judas should have known that Jesus would have forgiven him; there would probably have been no other consequence. After all, he had walked with Jesus and heard Him teach on how critical it was to forgive others. Unfortunately, Judas could not envision overcoming the remorse of his betrayal.

Handling Guilt

"To be" is the most irregular verb in the English language. In teaching us how to conjugate it, our elementary teachers explained that its proper form depends upon the point in time that one is referencing. For example, when referring to the *past,* one says, "I *was*"; the *present,* "I *am*"; and the *future,* "I *will be.*" None of these forms bears any resemblance to the others. How ironic...it reminds me of how we need to handle guilt. What I *was* (or did) yesterday does not define who I *am* today, and by the grace of God I will make smart choices and my future *will be* so glorious it may have no resemblance to my past or present.

> We must guard against feeling guilty over an action that is not a sin but rather a violation of our self-imposed values or standards.

To avoid allowing guilt to drive us to make a dumb decision, we must develop a sound strategy to defeat it before it has opportunity to become a stronghold in our minds. The suggestions below are sure steps to victory.

Determine whether you have actually done something wrong. During the 2009 Christmas holiday season, I (Deborah) had to resist feeling guilty when I decided not to purchase gifts for each of my 13 nieces and nephews. Why did I feel guilty? Because I had done so the previous year, and although I had the funds to do so again, I wanted to boycott the commercialization of this sacred holiday.

When guilt reared its head, I began my usual self-interrogation. The first thing I always ask is, *What did I do wrong?* Guilt is the feeling of regret over having committed a *wrongful* act. We must guard against feeling guilty over an action that is not a sin but rather a violation of our self-imposed values or standards. It is not a sin

- to say no to organizing your church's annual picnic even though you've done so for the past ten years

- to serve leftovers three times in one week because of your hectic work schedule

- to fail to pick up the restaurant tab for your unemployed friend who ordered everything on the menu as if she were having her last meal

- to refuse to make a personal loan to your irresponsible (or even responsible) friend.

None of these choices is a sin in the sight of God. Now, this does not mean that we have to take a black and white approach and only embrace values that would be a sin if violated. However, if you have unwisely elevated a *value* to the category of a *sin,* it's time to reevaluate how it is affecting the quality of your life.

Acknowledge the role others may have played in the situation. I was out of the city attending a women's retreat when my mom suffered a stroke several years ago. I started to beat myself up terribly. "If I had brought her along with me rather than deciding to fellowship with the ladies from my church (which I rarely had a chance to do), maybe it would not have happened." "If I had moved her into my home, she could have had better nutritional habits." The torrent of negative thoughts threatened to overwhelm me with guilt.

Guilt is one of the negative emotions I hate the most; therefore, I refuse to tolerate it. I started investigating the events leading up to the stroke. I learned that the person responsible for giving her her high-blood pressure medicine had not been consistent; my mom had been out of her prescription for over a week. Further, some other well-meaning relative had allowed her to eat several high-sodium tamales prior to the stroke. No way was I going to take responsibility for a consequence that was beyond my control.

I'm not recommending that you go on a fault-finding search for others to blame in order to assuage your guilt. I'm simply encouraging you not to immediately take full responsibility when other people or circumstances may have played a role.

Admit your role in sinful or unwise acts and repent for it. Taking responsibility for one's behavior is the hallmark of spiritual and emotional maturity. King David provides an excellent example. He was always quick to admit his role. Psalm 51 records his confession and repentance for committing adultery with Bathsheba:

> For I acknowledge my transgressions,
> And my sin is always before me.
> Against You, You only, have I sinned,
> And done this evil in Your sight.
> (Psalm 51:3-4)

(*Interpretation:* Lord, I'm not even going to try to justify my actions. I messed up. I sinned against You.)

He continued his contrite plea:

Create in me a clean heart, O God,
And renew a steadfast spirit within me.
Do not cast me away from Your presence,
And do not take Your Holy Spirit from me.
(Psalm 51:10-11)

(*Interpretation:* I'm sorry for the behavior that emanated from my evil heart. Fix me. I can't do this in my own strength. I need Your Spirit to survive.)

Accept God's forgiveness. Asking for God's forgiveness and accepting His forgiveness are mutually exclusive acts. Asking is easy; accepting can be also, but only if we really believe His Word. Most guilt-laden people feel more works are required for them to be truly forgiven. "Surely, we must offer more 'sacrifices,' do more penance." Not so. Here again, the words of King David ring loudly as a reminder:

For You do not desire sacrifice, or else I would give it;
You do not delight in burnt offering.
The sacrifices of God are a broken spirit,
A broken and a contrite heart—
These, O God, You will not despise.
(Psalm 51:16-17)

We can't sacrifice or earn our way into God's forgiveness. We must simply ask for it and receive it. Again I remind you, "when sins have been forgiven, there is no need to offer any more sacrifice" (Hebrews 10:18 NLT). All that God requires is the right attitude of the heart: genuine sorrow over the wrongful act and a sincere desire to do the right thing going forward. This is called *conviction* (versus guilt), and it is a positive response to sinful behavior. Peter, a disciple in Jesus' inner circle, denied he even knew Him—despite his earlier assertion that he was ready to die for Him. Nevertheless, he accepted Jesus' forgiveness and later became a miracle-working pillar in the early church.

Seek deliverance from feelings of guilt. "Wait," you might say, "I thought I was done." Not so fast. Even though you know and believe God has forgiven you, you need to pray against those feelings of guilt that try to keep you stuck in the wrongdoing. King David cried out, "Deliver me from the guilt of bloodshed." He knew that his merciful God would forgive him, but he wanted Him to eliminate the guilt that can linger long after we have repented. Don't tolerate it.

It can be humbling, healing, and honoring to God if, where possible, you admit your wrongdoing to those you may have harmed by your action. Ask their forgiveness. Don't worry about their response; that's between them and God. Where appropriate and possible, make every effort to restore what you took away.

Drown feelings of guilt by immersing yourself in the Word of God. Know that God is *all* about forgiveness. That's why He sent Jesus. Because we often refuse—or are reluctant—to forgive others, we try to bring God down to our level and assume He acts likewise.

I'd dare say that the majority of Christians do not fully grasp how ready God is to forgive us. If this is true in your case, it would be time well spent to meditate on and commit to memory passages such as the following:

- For You, Lord, are good, and ready to forgive, and abundant in mercy to all those who call upon You (Psalm 86:5).

- If we confess our sins, He is faithful and just to forgive us our sins and to cleanse us from all unrighteousness (1 John 1:9).

- So now there is no condemnation for those who belong to Christ Jesus (Romans 8:1 NLT).

- Then he says, "I will never again remember their sins and lawless deeds" (Hebrews 10:17 NLT).

- Just think how much more the blood of Christ will purify our consciences from sinful deeds so that we can worship the living God. For by the power of the eternal Spirit, Christ offered himself to God as a perfect sacrifice for our sins (Hebrews 9:14 NLT).

I encourage you today to open your eyes to how guilt is motivating you to make dumb choices and immobilizing you from serving God and fulfilling your destiny. Know that you can't serve God and guilt at the same time. It's no wonder David asked God to take away the guilt and then declared,

> *Then* I will teach transgressors Your ways,
> And sinners shall be converted to You.
> (Psalm 51:13, emphasis added)

Your Challenge

If you have repented of your sins but continue to be plagued with even occasional guilt, I challenge you to write out and meditate on the passage below in which the apostle Paul urged the Colossians not to allow guilt to mar their lives:

> This includes you who were once far away from God. You were his enemies, separated from him by your evil thoughts and actions. Yet now he has reconciled you to himself through the death of Christ in his physical body. As a result, he has brought you into his own presence, and *you are holy and blameless* as you stand before him *without a single fault.*
>
> But you *must continue to believe this truth and stand firmly in it.* Don't drift away from the assurance you received when you heard the Good News (Colossians 1:21-23 NLT, emphasis added).

Prayer

Father, thank You for Your amazing grace. You looked beyond my faults and saw my needs. When I confessed my sins, You were faithful and just to forgive me and to cleanse me from all unrighteousness. Because of the blood of Jesus, I am now free of condemnation. Guilt can no longer motivate me to make dumb choices. I will now press toward the mark for the prize of Your high calling for my life. In the name of Jesus, I pray. Amen.

Part 3

SEVEN
SECRETS
to a
GREAT DECISION

Chapter 15

CLEAR OBJECTIVES: ESTABLISHING WHAT YOU REALLY WANT

"If you chase two rabbits, both will escape."

Author unknown

SOMETIMES THE BOTTOM LINE for deciding what you really need is not always obvious. However, before you can begin to make a good decision, you must establish clarity about what you really want. For many, this can be a difficult task. Some people have put their desires on the back burner for so long they have abandoned all notions of a personal preference.

Bonita is a prime example. She is a single, 50-year-old elementary schoolteacher who has dedicated her entire life to being the backbone of her family and her community. When I (Deborah) spoke to her over a year ago, here is how our conversation went:

Bonita: "I want to retire from teaching next year, but I'm too young to just stop working altogether. I'd like to pursue some other endeavor afterward. However, I have no idea what that would be."

Me: "Well, what have you dreamed of doing or what do you think would bring you the most joy?"

Bonita: "You know (sigh), I honestly don't know what brings me joy.

I have invested the past 25 years into taking care of my ailing parents, rescuing irresponsible nieces and nephews, and catering to the needs of other family members. I haven't had the luxury of thinking about myself and what I really want. I just know that I want to do *something*."

Exasperated, I thought, *How will you ever decide what to do if you have no clue as to what you really want?* Our conversation sounded a lot like the thought-provoking scene in Lewis Carroll's classic children's tale, *Alice's Adventures in Wonderland.* Young Alice comes to a fork in the road and asks the Cheshire Cat which direction she should take.

> Clear objectives help you to frame your desires and prevent unwanted outcomes.

"That depends a good deal on where you want to get to," said the Cat.

"I don't much care where…," said Alice.

"Then it doesn't matter which way you walk," said the Cat.[1]

Advantages of Clear Objectives

Attempting to make a meaningful decision without clear objectives is as futile as trying to construct a house without a blueprint. Let's look at four major advantages of developing such objectives.

1. Clear objectives help you to frame your desires and prevent unwanted outcomes.

Consider the dilemma Sonya faced. She has a demanding job that requires frequent overtime and regular trips out of town. She has two teenage daughters. Her husband, Joe, is a stable father and tolerates her demanding career since it affords the entire family a host of luxuries.

Sonya's mother passed away five years ago and her 85-year-old father, Dan, lived alone in a neighboring city. His health was failing and he was diagnosed with early stages of dementia. As the only child and nearest relative, Sonya's choices were 1) hire full-time care for Dan in his home, 2) place him in a nursing facility, or 3) move him into her home with her family. She immediately ruled out the first option since the cost was prohibitive. Dan had always been a strong, independent man, and the idea of leaving his home would be a tough sell. Sonya's balancing act with her career and family was tenuous enough; the prospect of adding her father to the mix caused her much anxiety.

Before Sonya began to analyze her options, she stopped and came to grips with her primary objective: to ensure that her father received around-the-clock quality care. She had promised her mother on her deathbed that she would take care of him. Guilt over what she perceived as reneging on her promise started to invade her thoughts. But Sonya is a smart woman who is adept at balancing logic and her emotions. She stayed focused on her primary objective and did not allow guilt to override good judgment. She knew deep down that bringing her father into her already hectic household would be a dumb choice. Besides, with her schedule, the quality of his care would have been greatly compromised. Further, the quality of life for all the other family members would have been diminished.

After much research, she located a nice senior facility within 15 minutes of her home. It took Dan a few months to adjust to his new reality; however, he finally teamed up with a few war veterans and now he enjoys their daily fellowship. Sonya visits the center several times a week and has become acquainted with most of the personnel who care for Dan. Because she stayed focused on her primary objective—ensuring Dan's quality care—she made a smart decision.

2. Clear objectives focus your time and energy and facilitate the pursuit of your destiny.

Because Jesus performed many healings and other miracles, people were always seeking Him to meet their needs. Once when He was trying to have His daily quiet time with God, His disciples interrupted Him in response to the crowd's need for more miracles:

> Now in the morning, having risen a long while before daylight, He went out and departed to a solitary place; and there He prayed. And Simon and those who were with Him searched for Him. When they found Him, they said to Him, "Everyone is looking for You."

But He said to them, "Let us go into the next towns, that *I may preach* there also, because *for this purpose* I have come forth" (Mark 1:35-38, emphasis added).

Jesus easily made the choice to "go into the next towns" rather than catering to a crowd legitimately in need of miracles. Why? Because He was clear regarding His primary objective—to preach the gospel.

Clear objectives are especially critical in seeking employment. In a tight job market where you may be willing to consider just about any position, listing a vague objective on your resume, such as "growth and advancement" or "an environment where skills and experience can be utilized," can cause hiring managers to discount your potential.

Long gone are the days of the one-size-fits-all resume. The most effective resumes are targeted to a specific career goal. You have to be smart about this process. It is wise to develop several versions of your resume with different objectives. A good strategy is to search for jobs that appeal to you, review the job description, note the key credentials called for in the job placement ad, and then tailor your resume around it by highlighting your matching qualifications. As an example, a clear objective for a junior accountant position may be written along these lines:

> Objective: *An intermediate accounting position where advanced spreadsheet, budgeting, and analytical skills can enhance the company's profitability.*

3. Clear objectives minimize confusion when others are involved or will be affected by the outcome of a decision.

I once oversaw the donor contributions department of a large nonprofit organization. Even though the staff had to record information from thousands of donations, we all agreed that our objective was to keep the error rate under a specific percentage of our quarterly statements to the donors.

One quarter, after receiving a few too many calls about incorrect contribution statements, I called a meeting to find out the problem. The group's lead input clerk explained that the department had met its primary objective and had not exceeded the established error rate. I, however, had put my focus on the number of calls without regard to the total number of statements processed. We all had a stake in the outcome, which is why it's important to get group input and consensus in clarifying the objectives. As the leader, I wanted perfection. My motive was not totally for the glory of God, but partially to protect my reputation for excellence. It was humbling to learn that my pride had given me temporary amnesia about the clear objectives we had hammered out as a group. I apologized to the group and repented to God.

4. *Clear objectives can often help to redefine the real decision to be made.* Kevin Moriarity, business decision consultant, explains how:

> My wife and I moved this summer. At first we thought we had to decide which house to buy. As we talked about things more, we started to think about owning two homes, or a home and an RV. What started out as a relatively simple choice between homes became a much different decision about lifestyle. A clear definition of the objective, or the desired outcome of the decision, changed our alternatives. It changed the problem we were trying to solve by making a decision.
>
> To use a different example, perhaps you think you have to decide which college to attend. Is that truly the objective of your decision? Perhaps a trade school might be more suitable, or enlisting in the military, which would mean your objective is not to attend college, but to obtain an education. You won't really know until you give it some thought and be sure you know why you are making this particular decision.[2]

Your Challenge

With every significant decision you face, ask yourself, "What end result do I desire?" Or more importantly, "What end result does God desire?" Don't minimize this step for it will become the foundation for the other steps to a satisfying and rewarding outcome.

Prayer

Father, Your Word says that You will give me the desires of my heart if I delight myself in You. I ask that You cause me to desire Your will above all else. Reveal it to me and make clear paths for my feet as I acknowledge You in every decision. In the name of Jesus, I pray. Amen.

Chapter 16

CONCRETE INFORMATION: GETTING THE FACTS

"For which of you, intending to build a tower, does not sit down first and count the cost, whether he has enough to finish it?"

Jesus (Luke 14:28)

ENTREPRENEUR HARRY BROWN'S PROPOSAL to acquire X Company, a railcar manufacturer, appeared very promising to our small venture capital syndicate. It was certainly going to be a lot less risky than the recent string of unsuccessful entertainment industry startups we had pursued.

We were in dire need of a profitable investment. Far from glamorous, X Company was an established enterprise with a solid customer base—according to Harry. He and his partners planned to invest in new technology, rebrand the company's image, and take it to a whole new level. All they needed was expansion capital.

Harry had submitted an overwhelming amount of information on the company's history and its products. As part of our standard due diligence review of proposed investments, the syndicate selected me (Deborah) to perform an on-site review of the accounting records and other internal systems.

I flew into the midwestern city and settled in for my review. The first thing I asked to see was a listing of total sales by customer for the previous year. To my surprise, I discovered that over 65 percent of sales were routinely derived from a single source—Entity Y. To boot, according to X Company's accounts receivable records, Entity Y was extremely delinquent on its payments. Red flag. I then focused on investigating the financial strength of Entity Y. It soon became apparent that the company was in financial trouble.

With such a high risk of loss, our venture capital syndicate decided not to do the deal. Within one year of our decision, Entity Y filed bankruptcy and was completely out of business. We had made a smart choice by getting the *right* information.

During our informal Internet survey in which 240 respondents told us the dumbest choices they had ever made, one woman said she had invested in an enterprise without getting adequate information and had lost a significant amount of money. She is not alone. Many well-meaning, unsophisticated investors stop short of asking the right questions.

If you are not astute at researching and interpreting certain information, it is a wise move to hire someone who can do so for you. The biblical truth that "the just shall live by his faith" (Habakkuk 2:4) is no license to ignore the facts when making a critical decision. King Solomon, the sage of the Old Testament, admonished, "Buy the truth… also wisdom and instruction and understanding" (Proverbs 23:23).

A few years ago, I suffered a painful condition involving an inflamed jaw nerve. The medication the neurologist prescribed had many negative side effects that I was not willing to endure for the rest of my life. I researched possible remedies for over six months—from homeopathic cures to extreme surgeries. When I learned that a minimally invasive brain surgery had proven to be the most effective solution, I researched the best hospitals and brain surgeons to perform the task. Of course, I was standing in faith for divine healing from the inception of the pain, but I also know that God sometimes opts to heal through knowledgeable *medical* professionals rather than through a *miracle.* I believed that either way, healing ultimately rested in His hands. I submitted to the surgery and in record time was back in the saddle pursuing my destiny. Getting the right information helped me to make a wise choice.

The Role of Information

Information can be complex—sometimes too complex for nonexpert or inexperienced decision-makers to grasp. If you know you fall into such a group, you may need to cast aside your fear of looking stupid and ask that critical information be presented to you in a manner you can understand. Perhaps you are a *visual learner* and need to see a drawing, a PowerPoint graph, or other visual aid. Or you may be an *auditory learner* who comprehends information better by hearing it on CD or through brief explanations. The important thing is to admit your knowledge gaps and put steps in place to enhance your understanding.

If you are responsible for presenting information to others, never assume they prefer to receive it in the form that works best for *you*. Often when I'm explaining something technical to my husband (an auditory learner), I'll head for pencil and paper, and he'll say, "Just tell me." And when he's trying to help me understand the nuances of software programs, I'll ask, "Can you sketch it out for me?"

> In any decision, an abundance of data can weigh you down and diminish your capacity to come to a conclusion.

We must all learn to appreciate and cater to other people's learning styles—and to remember that one is not superior to the other. I find it helpful in the financial presentations I often make to nonexperts to combine the two styles and to keep the information concise enough for decision-makers to grasp it.

Paralysis by Analysis

Who hasn't heard that information is power? We live in the Information Age where we have instant access to knowledge, facts, analyses, and more data than we can ever digest. Although information is *power*, it can also spell *paralysis* when a decision-maker gets so bogged down in it he "can't see the forest for the trees." "Paralysis by analysis" can occur when you overanalyze the information or the circumstances you are faced with. When this happens, it can overwhelm you.

- "Should I pursue an advanced degree? I'm already forty years old. I'll be too old for a lucrative position by the time I finish the program."
- "Should I have the outpatient surgery to fix my torn rotator cuff? I don't want a surgery on my medical records; it may hinder me from getting insurance when I retire in a few years."
- "Should I buy or lease my next car?"
- "Should I sell my home now or wait for the real estate market to improve?"

In any decision, an abundance of data can weigh you down and diminish your capacity to come to a conclusion. Often, you must simply step back and assess the real issues of the proposed decision.

Ignoring the Facts

Sometimes in our personal and professional decision-making, our desires can cause us to simply ignore the facts. Consider Sally, who dated Wally for several years before he proposed. He was a handsome, charismatic entertainer; however, he had tons of emotional issues that were as evident as the baggage on an airport carousel. Sally had experienced his verbal abuse on many occasions. She saw his irresponsible financial behavior. Not only did *she* see it, her friends did also and urged her to sever the relationship with him. Wally's family even told her that she would be good for "helping him get his act together." Sally also knew, because of his irregular work habits, she would have to be the primary breadwinner. Nevertheless, against the advice of her friends, family members, and her own better judgment, she married him.

Wally has now successfully alienated her from her closest friends, forbidding her to contact them. He also continues the verbal abuse and intimidation. What caused Sally to overlook such glaring warning signs? Sally suffers from low self-esteem and loves the validation and prestige of "going home with the handsome man on the stage." Further, she rationalizes that she must "stick with her husband because he is sick"; she hopes that someday he will seek counseling. In the meantime, he has made her life a living hell, leaving her to grapple with the consequences of a really dumb choice.

I marvel at the senseless decision that many women (and men) make in committing to a lifetime partner with little or no information about his (or her) financial habits, emotional stability, family history, religious preferences, child-rearing philosophy, or other factors critical to a successful relationship. They often view quizzing a potential spouse about such matters a sign of mistrust. Quite the contrary; a lifelong choice should be an informed choice.

We have seen the consequences in other arenas of what happens when people ignore information or refuse to face facts. The major economies of the world came to the brink of collapse in early 2009 because hundreds of thousands of people obtained home loans that started out with teaser rates and graduated within two to three years to rates that made the loans unaffordable. Only God knows the driving emotions that overruled their logic.

When Bias Overshadows Information

Not only do we need to be on guard against turning a blind eye to critical data during the decision-making process, we should try to be aware of our personal biases. We must make every effort to evaluate information honestly, even if it challenges our biases, rationalizations, or stereotypes. It can be costly not to do so.

Such was the case with ABC-TV. In 1984, Bill Cosby, the highly popular black comedian, presented to ABC a proposal for a sitcom he'd created—and would star in—about an upscale black family. ABC turned him down, apparently "believing the show lacked bite and that viewers wouldn't watch an unrealistic portrayal of blacks as wealthy, well-educated professionals."[1] Cosby then presented the opportunity to NBC—and the rest is history. *The Cosby Show* remained the number one show for four straight years and was a ratings winner throughout its eight-year run. The show lifted NBC from its ten-year status as a last-place network to first place, resurrected TV comedy, and became the most profitable series ever broadcast.[2]

Information is routinely ignored in the world of politics. Princeton political scientist Larry Bartels analyzed survey data in the 1990s to prove that the majority of voters, without regard to their political party, consistently rationalize away any information they receive that is contrary to their entrenched beliefs about their party. According to Bartels, knowing more about politics doesn't erase partisan bias because voters tend to assimilate only those facts that confirm what they already believe. If a piece of information doesn't follow what they prefer to believe, it is conveniently ignored. "Voters think that they're thinking," Bartels says, "but what they're really doing is inventing facts or ignoring facts so that they can rationalize decisions they've already made." Once you identify with a political party, the world is edited to fit your ideology.[3]

Whether your bias is social, racial, or political, you would be wise to strive to maintain objectivity when making any decision.

Your Challenge

Is there a situation in your life where you are conveniently ignoring concrete information? If so, why? What are you afraid to acknowledge?

Prayer

Father, please give me the wisdom and the courage to obtain and face the facts of various situations in my life so that I may make informed decisions that will glorify You. In Jesus' name, I pray. Amen.

Chapter 17

CONTEMPLATION: WEIGHING RISKS AND REWARDS

"What we plant in the soil of contemplation, we shall reap in the harvest of action."

Meister Eckhart, German theologian

"GET YOUR SWORDS!"

These angry words spewed from David's mouth with no forethought of the consequences. He had sent a contingent of his men to request food from Nabal, a rich landowner. David felt he deserved Nabal's benevolence since he and his men had protected Nabal's sheepshearers from raiders and other perils when they had shared a common area in the wilderness. But Nabal was in a drunken state when David's men arrived; his response was harsh and crude:

> "Who is this fellow David?" Nabal sneered to the young men. "Who does this son of Jesse think he is? There are lots of servants these days who run away from their masters. Should I take my bread and my water and my meat that I've slaughtered for my shearers and give it to a band of outlaws who come from who knows where?" (1 Samuel 25:10-11 NLT).

When his men reported Nabal's reply, David became enraged. Of course, he was not in the best emotional state himself. After all, he had been on the run for some time from the insecure King Saul who, intimidated by David's victory over Goliath, sought to kill him. Further, Samuel the priest (who had already anointed David king-elect) had just died. Finally, David and his men had run out of food.

A popular drug recovery program admonishes its patrons to be on guard against becoming too *H*ungry, *A*ngry, *L*onely, or *T*ired. They must HALT and address their physical state as these conditions make a person more vulnerable to making a dumb choice. David was in this exact state. When his men reported Nabal's response, he ordered them to strap on their swords and join him in annihilating every man in Nabal's household.

> "A lot of good it did to help this fellow. We protected his flocks in the wilderness, and nothing he owned was lost or stolen. But he has repaid me evil for good. May God strike me and kill me if even one man of his household is still alive tomorrow morning!" (1 Samuel 25:21-22 NLT).

In the meantime, one of Nabal's shepherds rushed to Abigail, Nabal's wife, and reported how her husband had summarily dismissed David's men. He also gave her a positive account of the protection David and his men had given them during their sheepshearing season. She, being a woman of great wisdom and understanding, quickly loaded mules with generous provisions and headed out to intercept David. When she met him and his small army, she pleaded with him to reconsider the action he was planning to take. Her words were nothing short of brilliant, anointed, and prophetic.

> "I know Nabal is a wicked and ill-tempered man; please don't pay any attention to him. He is a fool, just as his name suggests. But I never even saw the young men you sent.
>
> "Now, my lord, as surely as the LORD lives and you yourself live, since the LORD has kept you from murdering and

taking vengeance into your own hands, let all your enemies and those who try to harm you be as cursed as Nabal is…

"When the LORD has done all he promised and has made you leader of Israel, don't let this be a blemish on your record. Then your conscience won't have to bear the staggering burden of needless bloodshed and vengeance. And when the LORD has done these great things for you, please remember me, your servant!" (vv. 25-26,30-31 NLT).

Abigail caused David to recognize his error in judgment. He called off the death raid and thanked her for her good sense and her intervention. The next day, Abigail related the entire incident to the now sober Nabal. Upon hearing it, he apparently had a heart attack or stroke and died ten days later. David sent for Abigail, and she became his wife.

Had it not been for the wise intervention of Abigail, this story would have been a prime example of what can happen when we don't take time to contemplate the full impact of our proposed actions. David knew that he would someday be king; yet, his physical and emotional state overrode any logic regarding how a senseless massacre would reflect on his dynasty. A decision made in haste can cause a lifetime of pain, remorse, and thwarted dreams.

Analyzing the Risks and Rewards

Whether it's a relational, financial, moral, or health dilemma, every decision has benefits (godly and ungodly) and trade-offs. For example, suppose that 49-year-old Talia has never married and yearns for companionship. John comes along and proposes to her. Although he is a fun-loving, Christian man, he is a horrible money manager. Should she ignore his financial habits for the sake of companionship?

What should Jesse do? He's just found in the local want ads a once-in-a-lifetime deal on the car of his dreams. However, he'll have to wipe out 75 percent of his savings to purchase it from the private owner.

When attempting to assess the risks and rewards of a course of action, we must consider objective and subjective issues. Here are some key questions that should help you to make a smart decision that balances facts and feelings:

- *How soon must I make the decision, and what is the biggest consequence of delaying it?* Having to do something instantly often leads to a bad choice. "Haste makes waste" may sound trite and worn, but the Bible says, "The plans of the diligent lead surely to plenty, but those of everyone who is hasty, surely to poverty" (Proverbs 21:5).

- *What impact will this decision have on the quality of my life tomorrow, next week, next month, and next year?* Will that double cheeseburger show up on the scale? Will the fancy new car triple my auto insurance premium? Will I have to live with the guilt of deception?

- *What impact will this decision have on the quality of life of those in my circle of love (family, friends) or circle of concern (employees)?* Will my wife leave me if she finds out? Will I have less time for my kids? How will this affect the bottom line?

- *Do the intangible benefits of my choice (peace of mind, happiness, more time with family) outweigh the tangible benefits (improved asset, luxury vacation)?* If I accept a less stressful position with lower pay, what lifestyle changes must I make?

- *What is the very worst thing that can happen for each alternative I consider?* Will my best friend resent me for informing her of her husband's flirtations?

- *What is the likelihood of it happening (based on experience)?* What is the success rate of this surgery? How safe is it to fly to the Middle East during these turbulent times?

- *How current and credible is the information that I am relying on to make the decision?* Are these financial statements prepared by an outside CPA or the owner's daughter? Is the input objective and verifiable, or is it simply the opinion of a close friend or relative?

- *Will this decision set an undesired precedent?* Have I locked myself into a recurring commitment, such as planning the annual picnic? Will others now feel it is okay to engage in a behavior toward me that I do not desire?

- *Would the choice I'm considering violate a biblical principle?* Will this decision cause me to have to tell or imply a lie?

- *Am I willing to say yes to God's choice in this matter, or do I have my mind fixed on what I desire?* Why shouldn't I marry Ted? I know I can change him. Besides, nobody is perfect.

Even though we have presented several questions above, such thorough analysis should not become an excuse for delaying or never making a final decision. It is critical, especially in business, to make timely decisions. What constitutes "timely" is debatable and the focus of scholar Paul C. Nutt's book, *Why Decisions Fail.* An article on Business Management Daily's website summarizes Nutt's perspective on timely decisions:

> While it's true that any decision is better than no decision, it's also true that during the 1990s, high-tech entrepreneurs created a myth that all decisions have to be made quickly. That myth, says Nutt, has seduced many leaders, leading to widespread errors across industries.
>
> In fact, Nutt points to research showing that only 1 in 10 decisions is urgent, and only 1 in 100 presents itself during a true crisis. Most of the time, you have time to reflect before deciding.
>
> What does Nutt mean by "time to reflect"? Probably more than days and less than months. Decisions that drag on for years usually fail, and that was true decades ago as well as today.
>
> It's probably worse now, Nutt says, because of the pressures that instant communication—the Internet, television, e-mail—bring.
>
> "If a problem is identified at 8:03, you're supposed to announce a solution by 8:05," Nutt says. "Having to do something instantly leads to a lot of bad decisions. And then, of

course, you have to focus your energy on justifying what you did."[1]

Good Idea or God Idea

I (Deborah) dated my husband only six months before we were married. I had sworn I'd never marry a man without dating him at least two years. Yes, I knew his family background since his brother is married to my first cousin, but I didn't really know him. The Lord simply showed me his heart and turned my heart toward him.

> Every decision involves facts and feelings, which may at times be at odds; however, there comes a time when *faith* must prevail.

At the time of this writing, we have been married 31 remarkable years. Coming from a broken family, I never fathomed I'd be married that long—especially not happily married. I relate this story to demonstrate that we can't confine our decision-making solely to a set of introspective questions and analyses. Neither can we allow our emotions to dictate our course of action. God has a plan and a destiny that trumps all our best musings.

> Many are the plans in a man's heart,
> but it is the LORD's purpose that prevails.
> (Proverbs 19:21 NIV)

Every decision involves facts and feelings, which may at times be at odds; however, there comes a time when *faith* must prevail. When you know beyond a shadow of a doubt that God has spoken to your heart, then it's time to stop the contemplation and just obey His leading.

> Trust in the LORD with all your heart,
> And lean not on your own understanding;
> In all your ways acknowledge Him,
> And He shall direct your paths.
> (Proverbs 3:5-6)

Your Challenge

1) What was the most recent decision that you made in haste, and what were the consequences of doing so?

2) Recall a time when you were too hungry, angry, lonely, or tired to make a smart choice (even a food choice). Resolve now that the next time you are tempted, you will acknowledge your emotional state and take smart steps to address it.

Prayer

Father, teach me how to wait in Your presence for Your leading. Help me not to lean to my own understanding of facts and information nor to let emotions cloud my judgment when making a decision. Help me to know when to simply walk by faith in spite of circumstances or my feelings. I want to glorify You in everything I do and say. In the name of Jesus, I pray. Amen.

CHAPTER 18

COUNSEL: UTILIZING THE POWER OF THE CAUCUS

*"Advise and counsel him; if he does not
listen, let adversity teach him."*

AN OLD PROVERB

I (RICKY) LEARNED MANY YEARS AGO as a young minister the benefit of surrounding myself with wise counselors, people who were more
experienced, more financially astute, and generally more knowledgeable than I. I solicited their input about everything from my marriage
to my ministering style. They spoke; I listened taking copious notes.

In addition to their advice, I made it a priority to research all types
of materials to help me make good decisions. Doing this allowed me to
better navigate my personal and business life in such a way that I could
avoid stupid, and costly, pitfalls. That's not to say I never made mistakes.
I did. However, my "village caucus" has been my eyes in areas of my life
where I've been very blind.

In 2007, I added a financial consulting team to my village caucus
for my church. This was one of the smartest business moves I have ever
made. They elevated my awareness of money and budgets. They gave
me insight on how to evaluate our staff's money management skills.

Finally, they helped me to implement a review system that keeps me clear about what is financially true and false about the ministry. Because we took their advice, when the economy dipped in 2008, we were armed. We had already streamlined our operation and upgraded our processes and procedures. Though revenues dipped, we were able to rebound and maintain positive cash flow.

The restructuring of our operation required humility, patience, sacrifice, and the courage to reinvent ourselves as a ministry. We made the hard decision to end our ministry's TV broadcast after 25 years. We then switched our focus to the Internet, which has proven to be far more profitable and effective. Because of our willingness to slash our expenses, we are now positioned for future prosperity.

Have you ever used a village caucus to help you make important decisions? Was your caucus effective, or did you discover that the members did not have the skills and wisdom to make a positive impact on your situation? In this chapter, we will look at people who have used a caucus—to their detriment or to their advantage. We'll see what an effective caucus should accomplish as well as show you how to develop such a group for yourself.

What It Means to Caucus

When the word *caucus* is used, the first thing that may go through your mind is the American political system. This word is commonly used to describe "a meeting between a group of selected individuals, often called delegates, who select the preferred party candidate to run for an election."[1] Usually the election in question is for the country's president. However, this term also can refer to a *guiding coalition*. This is the group that helps leaders decide the big issues and make the tough calls.[2] In both instances, the caucus is used to position the group for success.

A caucus comprises people with similar interests, but with a variety of expertise. The members are not all the same age, nor do they all have the same life story. A good caucus does not always agree with you. Instead, it should challenge you. To build an effective caucus, you should have the following elements: the right people, information, timing, level of focus, attitude, level of mental toughness, and a willingness to be open.

This formula has worked for several businesses including most recently Sears, which has now merged with Kmart because company leaders were looking for a fresh way to re-create the business. According to a recent article in the *Wall Street Journal:*

> A team of 180 e-commerce whizzes is searching for fresh ways to sell Kenmore appliances and Craftsman tools in an age of iPhone apps and Twitter. The group—a brain trust that includes veterans from Web stalwarts such as Amazon and Orbitz—is giving a digital makeover to Sears, the 124-year old merchant that rose to prominence on the strength of its eclectic mail-order catalog. Over the past 12 months, Sears Holdings Corp. has launched a flurry of Web sites and mobile-phone applications in an attempt to stretch sales beyond the physical borders of its aging stores.[3]

Sears executives understood that for the company to stay competitive, it had to change. Part of the company's plan was to invite the right outside experts to peer into its inner corporate sanctum. Because of company leaders' willingness to be open, Sears is now using the information to revamp how it does business in order to reach a techno-savvy audience.

> Plans go wrong for lack of advice; many advisors bring success.
> (Proverbs 15:22 NLT)

Effective Caucuses in Action

Businesses and other organizations have been using this model for decades. It's one of the tried-and-true routes to ensuring the entity has a long and profitable life. When we use an effective caucus for our lives, we can discover the quickest path to achieving our dreams. The wise words of Solomon state this sentiment even better. He wrote,

> Plans go wrong for lack of advice;
> many advisors bring success.
> (Proverbs 15:22 NLT)

Maxine learned this firsthand when she widened her village caucus. She was a working journalist by day and a creative storyteller by night. When she applied to graduate film school the first time, very few people read her writing sample. Consequently, she did not get accepted. Undaunted, she called the university to inquire why she had been turned down. A third-year grad student reviewed her portfolio and discovered she had not submitted a full-length screenplay. Though the application said a short story was acceptable, he told her that it was not preferred. Because Maxine believed in herself, the grad student offered to help her. Heartened, she then enlisted the help of her immediate supervisor and editing team. They agreed to read and edit her screenplay as well as write recommendation letters. After following her caucus's advice, Maxine resubmitted her writing portfolio the following year. By August, she had headed off to graduate school.

Unlike Maxine, Ben was adept at caucusing with a team. Therefore, when he decided to leave his cushy job as a publicist for a major firm to strike out on his own, he called me before making any moves. As we talked, Ben realized he hadn't considered a few major points: One, how his start-up company would financially support him over the next few years; and two, how his company would provide comprehensive health care for him and his family. To ensure that these things would be in place, Ben stayed at his job while building his public relations firm. Within 36 months, his consulting business overtook his day job. Now he has a thriving boutique public relations firm that employs five creative and satisfied people.

Maxine and Ben's lives changed because they allowed the right people with the right information at the right time to come into their lives. Both were focused on their goals, but flexible enough to alter their strategies if it meant bringing their dreams to fruition. Because Maxine and Ben felt secure in their abilities to accomplish their goals, their caucuses were not intimidating.

My wife and I have had our share of intense conversations about life, money, children, and all the other topics married couples discuss. But after 30 years, I am convinced that learning how to effectively caucus with her is one of my greatest accomplishments. It's allowed me to open up my life and my dreams. As a man, I had to get past the determination to always be right, to be the most knowledgeable, and so forth. In a nutshell, I had to understand there's power in not always being the smartest guy in the room. This is the ultimate strength of a caucus. As one management consultant likes to say, "None of us is as smart as all of us."

Pitfalls of an Ineffective Caucus

When you fail to follow sound advice, your dreams can be short-circuited. To understand this, take a look at the biblical story of Rehoboam, the son of King Solomon. He inherited a great caucus when his father died. His advisors experienced firsthand how King Solomon had run the kingdom during his 40-year reign. They helped build the Lord's temple and pay for the upkeep of the king's house. They witnessed his wise counsel throughout the land. They enjoyed a share in the wealth and safety his reign provided all the people. These advisors were the right people with the right information, and they were put in Rehoboam's life at the right time.

So when the young king faced his first major decision about how to rule the people, he held two caucuses: one with the elders, a seasoned caucus; and one with his friends, an untried caucus.

When he consulted with the elders, their advice was simple: "If you will be a servant to these people today, and serve them, and answer them, and speak good words to them, then they will be your servants forever" (1 Kings 12:7). Because of their experience, the elders knew what would endear Rehoboam to the nation. He needed to be a servant leader—someone open to hearing from the people, who would serve him faithfully.

Meanwhile, the younger caucus advised the young king to be harsher on the people than King Solomon:

Then the young men who had grown up with him spoke to him, saying, "Thus you should speak to this people who have spoken to you, saying, 'Your father made our yoke heavy, but you make it lighter on us'—thus you shall say to them: 'My little finger shall be thicker than my father's waist. And now, whereas my father put a heavy yoke on you, I will add to your yoke; my father chastised you with whips, but I will chastise you with scourges'" (1 Kings 12:10-11).

Unfortunately, Rehoboam rejected the elders' sound counsel and embraced the young men's foolish advice. When the people returned for Rehoboam's response to their request for relief from the heavy tax burden, he followed the script put forth by his peers. The people were incensed by his answer: "What share have we in David? We have no inheritance in the son of Jesse" (1 Kings 12:16).

That day Rehoboam lost the opportunity to head the entire nation. The northern ten tribes rejected Rehoboam's leadership. He reigned only over the "children of Israel who dwelt in the cities of Judah" (1 Kings 12:17).

This is a vivid example of how dreams, goals, and visions can be derailed or completely lost when we reject sound counsel to follow the advice of an untried caucus. Unfortunately, Rehoboam was not as smart as his grandfather King David, who surrounded himself with a team such as the men of Issachar "who had understanding of the times, to know what Israel ought to do" (1 Chronicles 12:32).

Often the difference between success and failure is what King Solomon admonished in his writings,

> Get wisdom! Get understanding!
> Do not forget, nor turn away from the
>   words of my mouth.
> Do not forsake her, and she will preserve you;
> Love her and she will keep you.
> Wisdom is the principal thing;

Therefore get wisdom.
And in all your getting, get understanding.
(Proverbs 4:5-7)

Your Challenge

If there is an area of your life that you want to improve, create a caucus following the steps below:

- Solicit the input of people who are more experienced and knowledgeable than you.

- Be honest about the facts of your life even when it hurts to do so.

- Listen to your caucus's advice though you may not totally agree.

- Weigh all your options, and then make a sound decision.

Prayer

Lord, thank You for surrounding me with helpful people. Give them the grace to advise me, and give me the grace to receive their advice. Guide me and be a lamp to my life. When this work is done, may I be able to say that You guided me and helped me create a path in places I could never have walked alone. In the name of Jesus, I pray. Amen.

CHAPTER 19

CREATIVITY: THINKING OUTSIDE-THE-BOX

"The world is but a canvas to the imagination."
HENRY DAVID THOREAU

CREATIVITY COMES FROM THE CREATOR. Pure and simple. Every human is endowed with the spirit of the Creator. Thus, there is no such thing as a person who lacks creativity; there are simply people who have not put forth the effort to allow it to spring forth.

I (Deborah) was over 30 years old before I fully embraced this wonderful truth. As a certified public accountant, I had always heard that accountants were not creative; they were "linear thinkers" who processed information in a straight, logical manner. I believed the stereotype. It worked just fine in my profession where I prepared financial statements, tax returns, and various quantitative analyses.

However, around the fourth year of our marriage, I became exasperated that I could think of nothing exciting to do to celebrate my husband's approaching birthday, even though he consistently found ways to surprise me. I finally said to him, "Look, you know that I'm an accountant and we are not creative people. I can't think of a thing to do beyond going out to dinner or having your friends over. Just tell me something that would be exciting, and I'll do it." He paused, gave me a long look, and said, "You mean to tell me that you have the spirit of the Creator dwelling in you and you cannot think of a creative way to celebrate my birthday?"

His question convicted my heart; it was an aha moment. Creativity doesn't emanate *from* me; it flows *through* me. Immediately, my affirmation became, "I am a creative person because the spirit of the Creator dwells in me." I can't tell you the number of times I have made this declaration and have seen God reveal insights and ideas beyond my imagination. Most of the people who know me say I'm creative. Who would have ever thought this would be the case for an accountant who had locked herself into an uncreative box?

That's what this chapter is about—learning how to "think outside-the-box" when making decisions. You may be asking, "What exactly is the meaning of this cliché?" The question is best answered by the illustration below. The challenge of this puzzle is to connect the dots using only four *straight* lines—without lifting the pencil.[1] Most of us will assume there is an invisible "no trespassing" boundary around the rows of dots. Thus, we think the puzzle must be solved within the confines of the square or imaginary box.

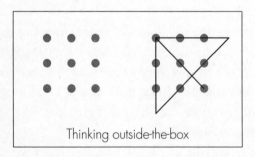

Thinking outside-the-box

However, as you can see from the solution to the right of the dots, one has to extend the lines *outside* the imaginary box to solve the puzzle. That's what thinking outside-the-box is all about, going beyond what is already established or what you already know, and pursuing untried and untested alternatives. It's the kind of thinking that led to the great inventions that have improved the quality of life for all humankind—from electricity to the telephone to airplanes.

Keys to Greater Creativity

Let's look at the essentials for tapping into your creative reservoir.

Fascination

Creative people don't run from or whine about adversity; they see problems as a normal part of living. They are fascinated by difficult issues, missing links, insurmountable odds, and impossible dilemmas. They are always asking *why not, why, what if, how can I improve, I wonder, suppose we started…or stopped,* or *how about…* These are great questions to entertain regularly if you want to be a more creative person. When you embrace God, you can claim His word: "I…dwell with prudence, and find out knowledge of witty inventions" (Proverbs 8:12 KJV).

Faith

To release your creativity, you must believe there is an answer to the problem at hand *and* that *you* have the ability to find it. Take King Solomon. God endowed him with great wisdom—because he asked for it (see 1 Kings 3:5-14). We saw him demonstrate it when two prostitutes came to court with a baby each claimed as her own. They were roommates and had each delivered a baby within three days of each other. One night Woman X accidentally smothered her baby by lying on him while they slept. She then switched her dead baby with Woman Y's baby.

Upon hearing the case, Solomon had to make a tough decision. There was no DNA testing in those days that would have easily identified the baby's natural mother. The new, inexperienced king called for a sword. He threatened to split the baby and give each woman one-half. Woman X was prepared to accept the decision (misery loves company), but Woman Y, out of love for her child, relented and asked the king to give the baby to Woman X. Solomon's out-of-the-box challenge revealed the true mother. He ordered the baby to be turned over

> Getting quiet and focused positions you for God to reveal His solution to a problem.

to Woman Y. News of this creative judgment spread throughout the kingdom and confirmed his extraordinary wisdom (see 1 Kings 3:16-28).

When we have faith that God can solve our dilemmas, He will show Himself strong in our lives.

Focus

Revelations rarely come in the midst of hustle and bustle and the distractions of phones, emails, and fast-paced living. I know this from experience and must constantly remind myself of this truth. A quiet mind is a receptive mind. Getting quiet and focused positions you for God to reveal His solution to a problem.

Often when I find myself trying to meet a publishing deadline and feeling mentally drained, I abruptly stop my frantic research, email solicitations, and all self-efforts. I lift my hands high into the air in complete surrender and pray, "Father, this is *Your* project. Reveal to me now the life-changing truths You want me to include in *Your* book." It seems that in no time, I am experiencing Ephesians 3:20-21: "Now to Him who is able to do exceedingly abundantly above all that we ask or think, according to the power that works in us, to Him be glory."

Flexibility

Nothing enters a closed object—especially a closed mind. Therefore, we must not be fixated on a traditional or historical approach to a problem. Rather, we must stay open to all possible solutions based on available information and tools.

At a retreat I once attended, the session leader, Mike, placed an empty champagne glass on our table of eight and asked us to list as many possible uses for the glass as we could imagine. At first, we put forth a few traditional suggestions: use as a juice glass, cottonball holder, safety-pin holder. Soon we were stumped. These, Mike explained, represented our "inside the box" ideas. He then challenged us to expand our minds and to think of more applications. We eventually recorded over 80 uses, including cookie cutter, centerpiece holder for a small table, and more.

The exercise reminded me of the popular 80s TV show, *MacGyver*. Angus MacGyver was an easygoing secret agent who didn't carry a gun, but who ingenuously turned everyday materials into weapons that got him out of trouble. He kept an open mind about the use of any object that came across his path. We tuned into the show each week to see his creativity.

Fearlessness

In decision-making, the urgency or magnitude of a problem can push us into a creative mode—that is, if we refuse to become paralyzed with doubt or fear of the outcome of a potential solution. The old adage "necessity is the mother of invention" applies here. A need often forces people to invent things or to give birth to creative alternatives.

The story of Jacob demonstrates this principle. Genesis 29–30 records how his uncle Laban promised his younger daughter, Rachel, to Jacob in return for seven years of labor, only to trick him into marrying the older, less attractive daughter, Leah, instead. Jacob willingly served another seven years in exchange for the right to marry his beloved Rachel. Then, Jacob put himself in a precarious position when he negotiated his compensation package with his dishonest and unfair employer. He asked that his pay consist only of spotted and striped sheep and goats; all of the more favorable white or solid animals would belong to Laban. The greedy uncle heartily agreed. However, that same day Laban removed all the spotted and striped sheep and goats from the herd. But God's hand of favor was upon Jacob, and his creative juices started to flow:

> Jacob, however, took fresh-cut branches from poplar, almond and plane trees and made white stripes on them by peeling the bark and exposing the white inner wood of the branches. Then he placed the peeled branches in all the watering troughs, so that they would be directly in front of the flocks when they came to drink. When the flocks were in

heat and came to drink, they mated in front of the branches. And they bore young that were streaked or speckled or spotted (Genesis 30:37-39 NIV).

Jacob's strategy yielded him a large speckled and spotted herd, and he became even more prosperous. You can't keep a fearless, creative man down.

Avis Rent a Car is an example of corporate creativity. For about 13 years the company had been in the red, sorely lagging behind Hertz, the industry's number one rental car company. In 1962, its then new president, Robert C. Townsend, hired the Doyle Dane and Bernbach (DDB) ad agency. Bill Bernbach bluntly told Townsend that Avis needed to overhaul its customer service because, as Bernbach put it, "It's always a mistake to make good advertising for a bad product."[2]

Avis revamped its offerings; DDB spent 90 days researching Avis's strengths. The outcome was phenomenal. Using the slogan, "Avis Is Only No. 2, We Try Harder,"[3] DDB built a campaign from Avis's place of strength—"trying harder" than its competition to please its customers. DDB's creativity was the impetus for Avis to become a leading global rental car company.

Fortitude

Creative people have the fortitude to see their ideas come to fruition—no matter how much disappointment or discouragement they encounter. After many challenges to his patent, Alexander Bell could have given up. He offered the patent for the *telephone* to Western-Union for $100,000. They declined. "This 'telephone' has too many shortcomings to be seriously considered as a means of communication. The device is inherently of no value to us." This excerpt from a Western-Union 1876 internal memo shows the lack of creativity of its management. Bell finally found willing backers and formed his own company. The telephone patent has been estimated as the most valuable patent of all time. Bell's Company, AT&T, later acquired Western-Union.[4]

Apple Computer cofounder Steve Jobs also tells of his frustration in attempting to get Atari and Hewlett-Packard interested in the personal computer he and Steve Wozniak developed:

> So we went to Atari and said, "Hey we've got this amazing thing, even built with some of your parts, what do you think about funding us? Or, we'll give it to you. We just want to do it. Pay our salary, we'll come work for you." And they said, "No." So then we went to Hewlett-Packard and they said, "Hey, we don't need you; you haven't even got through college yet."[5]

Jobs and Wozniak persevered and found receptive investors. As of February 2010, Apple boasted a net market value of over $177 billion.[6]

Your Challenge

- As an exercise to develop your creativity, find a simple everyday object (a utensil, paper clip, bookend, etc.) and try to think of all the practical applications it could have.

- If you are facing a problem in which traditional solutions are not feasible, find a quiet place to get focused and ask God to reveal a solution. Meditate on Daniel 2:20-22 as you wait for His answer:

> "Blessed be the name of God forever and ever,
>   For wisdom and might are His...
> He gives wisdom to the wise
> And knowledge to those who have understanding.
> He reveals deep and secret things;
> He knows what is in the darkness,
> And light dwells with Him."
>   (Daniel 2:20-22)

Keep pen and paper nearby and be ready to write down the thoughts that come to mind.

Prayer

Father, I acknowledge You as the Creator of everything. Every good and perfect gift comes from You. Thank You that Your Spirit dwells in me and empowers me to conceive solutions and worthy alternatives to the issues, problems, and dilemmas in my life and in society at large. I know that apart from You I can do nothing, so I give You all the honor and the glory. In the name of Jesus, I pray.

CHAPTER 20

COURAGE: IMPLEMENTING THE DECISION

*"Courage is the first of human qualities because
it is the quality which guarantees the others."*

ARISTOTLE

STARTING A NEW BUSINESS after the first one failed. Taking another management position after being fired elsewhere. Going back to college after flunking out the first semester. Getting pregnant again after experiencing a miscarriage.

Courage. It's generally described as the mental, emotional, and physical strength to resist opposition, danger, or hardship. It's having the heart to face then overcome any opposition with keen mental, emotional, and physical abilities. Speaker, seminar leader, and courage coach Sandra Ford Walston elaborates:

> Great leaders throughout history have acted from their hearts, but the definition of courage has been narrowed to simple heroics. Courage, however, means a lot more, and it is key for each one of us. According to Aristotle, courage is the first human virtue because it makes all of the other virtues possible.[1]

Courageous people are everyday folks who, when the time came, chose to face their giants and not run. They are imperfect people who admitted their failures, yet still chose to start all over.

When I (Ricky) think about courage, I think about Brenda. When she was 27, she dreamed of going to college. But before she could embark on her lifelong passion, she had a choice to make: Stay with an abusive and philandering husband, or divorce him and uproot her two children to start over elsewhere. The choice may sound simple, but at the time, Brenda had only a high school education. She had worked only menial jobs. In addition, she had been married for 10 years. She wondered if she could provide a good life for her children. She wondered if she could be a good parent alone. She wondered if she could do this without the possible assistance of her husband's extended family. She wondered if she could ever trust and love another man again. She wondered...and wondered...

Swallowing her doubts, she divorced her husband because of his unfaithfulness and because she believed that her life without him would be better than her life with him. It was a bold, gutsy move she never regretted. Because she left, she was free to get her undergraduate degree, start her wedding planner business, and remarry. It wasn't easy. It took work, faith, and guts. But now she is whole again.

Are there some areas in your life that you know you need to change, but you are afraid? Need a boost of courage? Keep reading. We'll peek into the lives of people who have faced their giants and see what lessons we can learn from their experiences.

Uncovering Courage

A few commonalities are found among people who, when faced with life-changing moments, decide to be courageous:

- They face the challenge.
- They reveal their vulnerabilities about the issue.
- They probe the facts.

- They discern the real problem.

- They discover alternative solutions.

- They create multiple plans.

- They act, taking the risk.

This list is by no means exhaustive; however, it is a good foundation of how one goes about making a courageous decision. This list has been used in business time and time again.

Joel Michael Evans is a community college professor who teaches students how to make the tough calls in a business setting. Along with the above list, he says that most decisions boil down to the following: identify the problem, make a decision, and then justify your actions. This approach empowers students to make good decisions in business and in life.[2]

Most people make decisions according to how they *feel*. However, to make a courageous choice in the midst of a serious challenge, more than feelings are required. You must be able to gather the facts, sift through the consequences of the risks, and then take the risk, being able to point to your reasons why you made the choice. Courage, therefore, is the power behind the action of the choice.

In 1985, Apple Computer cofounder Steven Jobs was in the midst of a painful power struggle for his company. Jobs had been fired from the day-to-day operations but left as chairman of the board and a major stockholder. His reduced role led him to start another company. Some board members believed his new company would compete with Apple products and considered legal action. The then 30-year-old multi-millionaire had to make the inevitable choice to either fight for his company or let go and start over elsewhere. He resigned. In his resignation letter, he stated: "I am but 30 and want still to contribute and achieve."[3]

Here is a man who courageously let go of what he created to be free to try again. Jobs started the NeXT Corporation, which Apple bought in 1996, and regained his position as CEO of Apple by 2000.[4] Since then, Jobs has lit a creative fire at the company to include products such as the iPod in 2001, iTunes in 2003, and iPhone in 2007. If that weren't enough, he did most of this while facing pancreatic cancer, which ultimately led to his liver transplant in 2009. At the time of this writing, Jobs worked at Apple part-time.

Being courageous isn't just for the boardroom. God repeatedly tells us throughout the Bible to be strong and of good courage. It was his command to Joshua after the death of Moses. Joshua picked up the mantle to lead the children of Israel over the Jordan and into the Promised Land. Finally, after 40 years of wandering, God was allowing the Hebrews to enter the land that flowed with milk and honey.

This was not an easy task. Formidable opponents still occupied the Promised Land, and Joshua was a new leader. Anytime there is change, great courage becomes vital. God gave Joshua implicit instructions about the land, the fate of his opponents, and the blessings that inure from following His law to the letter (Joshua 1:4-9). It's interesting to note the number of times God reiterated in this passage the importance of being courageous:

- "Be strong and of good courage…" (v. 6)
- "Only be strong and very courageous…" (v. 7)
- "Have I not commanded you? Be strong and of good courage; do not be afraid…" (v. 9)

God didn't *make* Joshua courageous; He simply gave him some promises and instructions, and challenged him to be so. Joshua rose to the occasion. So can we if we rely on His promises and follow the instructions in His Word.

Pushing Past Courage Blockers

I believe that much of the success Brenda, Steven, and Joshua achieved is attributable to their pushing past what I call courage blockers: loss, insecurity, failure, emotions, unforgiveness, and narrow-mindedness. These six obstacles tend to force people to put the brakes on their dreams.

However, if you resist the urge to succumb to these blockers, you will achieve your goal.

Anytime I face huge obstacles, I remember the story of the four lepers described in 2 Kings 7:3-10. These men had the courage to venture outside their condition to save themselves and ultimately all of Israel. During this time, Syria had besieged Samaria—an ancient city in central Palestine. The war was so great that Samaria and all the land surrounding it experienced famine. In the midst of this, four leprous men sat at the entrance of the city gate. They were forced by law to live isolated lives. The isolation severed their ties with all family and friends. The *loss* of community ties, the *insecurity* of their futures, and the *emotions* of the moment overwhelmed them. But instead of being overcome by those courage blockers, they pushed past them to entertain a bold life decision:

> "Why are we sitting here until we die? If we say, 'We will enter the city,' the famine is in the city, and we shall die there. And if we sit here, we die also. Now therefore, come, let us surrender to the army of the Syrians. If they keep us alive, we shall live; and if they kill us, we shall only die" (2 Kings 7:3-4).

Deciding to enter the enemy's camp rather than wait for death was their first courageous step. Their next step was to implement the plan. So they waited until twilight before going to the Syrian camp. Upon entering, they found the camp deserted. As they inspected the area, they discovered that the Syrian army had left behind everything: horses, donkeys, food, silver, gold, and clothing. Unbeknown to them, God had caused the Syrian army to hear the rumblings of a mightier army at twilight—around the same time the four men were coming to the camp—and the Syrians had fled for their lives, leaving everything behind.

Though the men began to plunder the spoils, they stopped because they realized this should be a shared victory for all of Israel. So they went back to the city and told the gatekeepers everything. Word reached the king, and he then sent scouts to check out the story. Finding it true, the people of Israel plundered the Syrian camp, ending the famine.

This was a mighty moment where guts and courage paid off. Ironically, or perhaps we should say providentially, both the lepers and the Syrians arose and left at twilight. Twilight is a time when there is as much darkness as there is light. At times you may have to move out in faith despite the unknown perils of the darkness. You can be one knock away from a new job or a question away from a promotion and raise. All you have to do is press past the courage blocker of former *failure* to get to the new blessings courage offers.

Another benefit these men experienced was forgiveness. Instead of being *unforgiving,* which is a courage blocker, they chose instead to look beyond how they were treated by the people of Israel because of their leprosy and share the spoils of the Syrian camp. Doing so also meant they didn't succumb to the courage blocker of *narrow-mindedness.* On the contrary, they widened their vision; thus they were part of God's bigger plan to end the nation's famine and helped secure the people's survival.

Discovering the Courage Within

As the leader of a large ministry, I am constantly called upon to make tough choices. To encourage myself, I often repeat the words the apostle Paul wrote to Timothy, "For God has not given us a spirit of fear and timidity, but of power, love, and self-discipline" (2 Timothy 1:7 NLT). Repeating this Scripture allows me to remember that because of Christ, I am adequately equipped to carry out the task at hand.

One of the significant benefits of exercising our courage is that it inspires others. Billy Graham once said, "Courage is contagious. When a brave man takes a stand, the spines of others are stiffened."[5] We never know

> "Courage is contagious. When a brave man takes a stand, the spines of others are stiffened."
> —Billy Graham

who's watching us. So be courageous. Make smart choices, and watch your life and the lives of your observers improve.

Your Challenge

If you're ready to take your courage to new heights, try the following strategies:

- Do something you're afraid to do: Go back to school. Start a business. Try a new outdoor sport.

- Stop avoiding confrontation. If you know you need to speak the truth to someone, do so in love and stop putting it off.

- Get out of your comfort zone. If you have an unfulfilled dream, maybe it's time to dust it off, create a plan, and get moving.

Prayer

Lord, I confess I have allowed people or circumstances to block my advancement. With Your help, I will not permit loss, insecurity, failure, emotions, personal injustice, or even my narrow-mindedness to rule my life. These things block my courage and prevent me from moving forward to face my challenges. Today, I look for other alternatives and dare to act upon them. I know that apart from You, I am vulnerable and headed for defeat. But with Your strength, I am strong and courageous. Nothing shall be able to defeat me all the days of my life. In the name of Jesus, I pray. Amen.

CHAPTER 21

CLEAN CONSCIENCE: EXPERIENCING
PEACE WITH YOUR CHOICE

*"Conscience is the root of all true courage; if a man
would be brave let him obey his conscience."*

JAMES FREEMAN CLARKE

CONSCIENCE. IT'S THAT LITTLE VOICE in the back of your mind. It's the spiritual compass guiding your choices. It's your gut telling you to do the right thing. Whatever you call it, the conscience is the value meter that gauges your behavior.

We equate conscience with things we've done because we believed they were the right things to do. This includes things we've done because we believed that if we didn't, our lack of action would *be on our conscience.* These experiences vary from person to person and are based on our individual moral standards. Kenneth E. Goodpaster, chairman of business ethics at the University of St. Thomas in Minneapolis, Minnesota, described the conscience as "our primary check on the unbalanced pursuit of goals and purposes."[1] This primary check works without fail as long as we do not compromise our moral standards.

This is a lesson Josephine experienced in college. She was a quiet young woman with a desire to experiment and taste life for herself. She wanted to be the best at whatever she tried: sports, academics, ministry, auto mechanics—everything. She hailed from a small town and was from a solid church-going family. Of the many sermons she heard on Sunday mornings, the one that stuck with her the most was the importance of living with a clear conscience. Her pastor had said that the best way to have a clear conscience is to develop a strong moral code, and then heed the gentle nudging in your heart. Otherwise, he cautioned, compromise of her moral code would deaden her conscience. To help solidify his words, she memorized 1 Timothy 4:2 (NLT): "These people are hypocrites and liars, and their consciences are dead." She never wanted to be among those with a dead conscience.

Such was the lesson she took with her when she left home for a Big Ten university. She met new people and made new friends. Then she encountered new distractions. Sometimes her friends wanted to sample alcohol, try pot, engage in sex, and a host of other activities contrary to her moral code. It was hard being labeled the "good girl." However, she had made a pact with herself that she would live with a clear conscience. She would do the right thing even if it made her unpopular. It was a hard stance to take. However, by her senior year, her friends respected her decision and often consulted her when they had problems or needed a morality check.

Josephine learned that she didn't have to change the core of what she believed to be accepted. Instead, she inspired her friends to strengthen their moral resolve. Her story is like so many others who have refused to waver on their beliefs.

What about you? Do you strive to maintain a clear conscience at all times? Is there a crucial decision you need to make, but need a boost in the right direction? Let's explore the hard choices others have made.

Seared Conscience Versus a Pure Conscience

According to Alan S.L. Wong, the "conscience is not an infallible guide to behavior because it works according to the standards we have adopted."[2] Our conscience is fluid. As we learn, we grow. As we experience, we change—and hopefully mature.

Our moral standards reflect this process. Over time, we embrace the moral standards that we determine not to violate. This code becomes the measuring stick for our consciences to know right from wrong. The moment we develop bad moral habits, we deaden or sear our conscience. A seared conscience cannot feel. This happens when we continually do the wrong thing. Eventually, the *wrong* thing becomes the *normal* thing in our life skewing our moral compass. The prophet Isaiah strongly warned against developing such a mindset:

> Woe to those who call evil good, and good evil;
> Who put darkness for light, and light for darkness.
> (Isaiah 5:20)

The apostle Paul described this deadening in a letter to the church at Ephesus. He warned the new Christians about allowing their lives to slip into that state:

> This I say, therefore, and testify in the Lord, that you should no longer walk as the rest of the Gentiles walk, in the futility of their mind, having their understanding darkened, being alienated from the life of God, because of the ignorance that is in them, because of the blindness of their heart; who, being *past feeling,* have given themselves over to lewdness, to work all uncleanness with greediness (Ephesians 4:17-19, emphasis added).

The pitfalls of having a seared conscience means you understand nothing, you are alienated from God, your heart is hardened, and you are unfeeling. Instead, you revel in all things that produce greed, feed lust, and corrupt the mind.

> The main benefit of having a pure conscience is that your life remains foundationally solid.

On the flip side, a pure conscience means you live free from guilt. You know your conscience works because, when you cross your moral standards, you feel remorseful. You will do everything to ensure you don't overstep those personal boundaries.

To help achieve this, you seek forgiveness, quickly forgive, and then let the offense go. You have built strong moral standards that value integrity, honesty, and truth. Having a pure conscience was so critical that the apostle Paul reiterated its importance to young Timothy in the early part of his ministry:

> Timothy, my son, here are my instructions for you, based on the prophetic words spoken about you earlier. May they help you fight well in the Lord's battles. Cling to your faith in Christ, and keep your conscience clear. For some people have deliberately violated their consciences; as a result, their faith has been shipwrecked (1 Timothy 1:18-19 NLT).

The main benefit of having a pure conscience is that your life remains foundationally solid. Josephine demonstrated this when she would not violate her moral standards for friendship. By retaining her values, she gained her friends' respect and her reputation remained unblemished.

Your conscience also remains pure when you exercise it on behalf of someone else. As a youngster, my friends and I (Ricky) used to go to the 99-cent movie theater. One Saturday as we were about to leave the theater, we noticed a man sleeping in the last row. His mouth was wide open. One of my friends thought it would be funny to drop a cigarette down his throat. Shocked, my conscience screamed, *Do something.* I quickly grabbed my friend's hands. He looked at me and exclaimed, "Party pooper. That is all you are is a party pooper." I didn't care. Hurting someone else for my enjoyment was not my idea of fun. It was wrong, and there was no way I was going to allow my friend to violate that principle—at least not on my watch. That day I followed my conscience, and I'm still proud to say I did.

Good Conscience in Action

Someone once said, "It's not hard to make decisions when you know what your values are." The Bible is replete with stories of people who refused to violate their conscience and willingly paid the price for doing so.

Genesis 39 records the story of Joseph, the Hebrew slave clearly on a career fast-track as the household manager for Potiphar, the head of security in Egypt. He rejected the sexual advances of Mrs. Potiphar, and it cost him his freedom. He explained his conviction this way: "How then can I do this great wickedness, and sin against God?" (Genesis 39:9).

Daniel refused to put his prayer life on hold when his envious coadministrators convinced the king to issue an edict forbidding anyone to petition any god or man for 30 days (Daniel 6). When they found Daniel offering his regular prayers to God, they promptly tossed him to the lions. God miraculously shut the lions' mouths and he suffered no harm.

Daniel's God-fearing friends, Shadrach, Meshach, and Abed-Nego, refused to bow to a golden image the king had set up (Daniel 3). Even the threat of being thrown into a fiery furnace did not cause them to compromise; they maintained their resolve to never worship anyone except God. They explained to the furious king, "our God whom we serve is able to deliver us from the burning fiery furnace, and He will deliver us from your hand, O king. But if not, let it be known to you, O king, that we do not serve your gods, nor will we worship the gold image which you have set up" (Daniel 3:17-18). Although they were indeed thrown in the furnace, the fire had no power over them. They walked out without even the smell of smoke on their clothing.

All these individuals held fast to their convictions because they placed a high value on their relationship with God. In every instance, He rewarded their faith with great promotions.

Developing a Strong Conscience

Here are four keys to being at peace with your conscience and your choices:

- Choose clear-cut life principles. These are moral standards you will not violate. These direct the course of your life.
- Set clear priorities that you will not abandon. These are your

do-or-die tasks that must be accomplished first. They are part of your daily life.

- Make yourself accountable to your village caucus. They will help support your values.

- Remove yourself from old environments that reinforce bad habits.

These keys, coupled with other strategies we have recommended throughout this book, will help you develop a strong conscience.

This became a reality for Yvonne. With tears in her eyes, she decided that she would not cover for her husband, Jeff. He had done irreparable damage to his family. It's amazing that his misdeeds had gone undetected for so long. After the police arrested him, several other victims came forward. Yvonne had been married for 20 years. She was a homemaker with little job training and had four children to help get through school. However, her conscience troubled her. She may have been madly in love with Jeff, but this she could not ignore.

During the one-week child-molestation trial, Yvonne sat horrified listening to the details of his exploits with various children, including their oldest daughter, who courageously told her story. The details were ugly, and they hurt. Yet, Yvonne had no doubt in her mind that turning Jeff in was the right thing to do. She did not know how she would support her family, but at that moment it wasn't important. All that mattered was that her child knew she believed her.

The verdict came back guilty on all counts of aggravated child molestation. Due to the repeated brutality of the crimes and the number of victims involved, Jeff was sentenced to 25 years in prison without parole. When it was all over, Yvonne hugged her daughter.

"I love you, baby," Yvonne whispered.

"Thank you for believing me, Mama," her daughter whispered back.

The two left the courtroom ready to envision a new life. Yvonne held her head up. She had made a smart choice. Her conscience was clear, and her daughter was safe.

Your Challenge

- Identify an area of your life in which you struggle to maintain a clear conscience.
- List the possible consequences of succumbing to that temptation.
- What are the rewards for doing the right thing?
- Pray the prayer below when you are tempted to violate your conscience.

Prayer

Lord, I want to live my life with a clear conscience. I can draw near to You with a sincere heart and receive full assurance and faith. You said my heart could be sprinkled clean of an evil conscience by the blood of Christ. I claim this for my life today. These issues that challenge me will no longer have power in my life. By Your power, I am at peace and will live with a clear conscience from this day forward. In the name of Jesus, I pray. Amen.

EPILOGUE

OUR DECISIONS REVEAL our values, our intellect, and yes, our faith. They determine the quality of our lives. They require obedience to and dependence upon God. They demand wisdom and courage. Joan of Arc, the brave peasant girl credited with saving the French from English domination, said, "One life is all we have, and we live it as we believe in living it."

All of us have dreams of a productive and fulfilling life; nobody wants his life to be a waste of time. Our greatest challenge is to develop a strong, biblically based belief system that becomes the foundation for all our choices. Taking the time to learn what God has to say about morality, relationships, finances, or health is the first step in redefining our lives. Courageously reviewing our belief systems can be a defining moment that unleashes new potential.

We hope the principles, stories, personal challenges, and prayers in this book will give you a solid foundation for making smarter choices. We highly recommend that you commit to an accountability circle of friends, family, or colleagues who will talk to you honestly about the anger, fear, greed, impatience, stress, curiosity, lust, pride, insecurity, guilt, or other factors that have driven you to make dumb choices. This could prove to be one of the most productive endeavors in your life.

We challenge you to begin daily to practice the secrets to a great decision: clarify your objectives, get the facts, weigh the risks and rewards, utilize the power of a wise caucus group, think outside-the-box, and be at peace with your choice. Most of all, exercise courage and implement your decision. Theodore Roosevelt cautioned, "In any moment of decision, the best thing you can do is the right thing, the next best thing is the wrong thing, and the worst thing you can do is nothing."

You can stop being a victim of your indecisiveness. Understand that even when you decide to "wait upon the Lord" and to let Him bring His will to pass, these are very proactive and powerful choices to avoid the pitfalls of a hasty decision. However, do not hide behind waiting on God as an excuse for inaction. There comes a time to exercise faith and pursue unknown territory.

By the power of God, you can develop into a decisive and courageous person who makes smart choices not determined solely on intellect, facts, and analyses nor solely on emotions. You will seek God's will and arrive at the right choice—His choice. Therefore, whether you are the chief financial officer of a corporation or the chief family officer (patriarch, matriarch, go-to person) among your relatives, know that you will make a winning decision if you acknowledge the Lord in all your ways and allow Him to direct your paths.

Some decisions may not initially appear to be winners, but know that your heavenly Father sees your yesterdays, todays, and tomorrows all at once, and He has plans for you just as He had for His people in exile in Babylon: "For I know the plans I have for you," says the LORD. "They are plans for good and not for disaster, to give you a future and a hope" (Jeremiah 29:11 NLT). We must simply,

> Trust in the LORD with all your heart;
>> do not depend on your own understanding.
> Seek his will in all you do,
>> and he will show you which path to take.
>> (Proverbs 3:5-6 NLT)

SCRIPTURES FOR DIVINE GUIDANCE

Show me the right path, O Lord;
    point out the road for me to follow.
Lead me by your truth and teach me,
    for you are the God who saves me.
All day long I put my hope in you.
                (Psalm 25:4-5 NLT)

I will instruct you and teach you in the way
    you should go;
I will guide you with My eye.
                (Psalm 32:8)

Teach me to do your will,
    for you are my God.
May your gracious Spirit lead me forward
    on a firm footing.
                (Psalm 143:10 NLT)

Trust in the Lord with all your heart,
And lean not on your own understanding;
In all your ways acknowledge Him,
And He shall direct your paths.
                (Proverbs 3:5-6)

Your word is a lamp to my feet
And a light to my path.
                (Psalm 119:105)

For You are my rock and my fortress;
Therefore, for Your name's sake,
Lead me and guide me.
(Psalm 31:3)

Look straight ahead,
    and fix your eyes on what lies before you.
Mark out a straight path for your feet;
    stay on the safe path.
Don't get sidetracked;
    keep your feet from following evil.
(Proverbs 4:25-27 NLT)

If you need wisdom, ask our generous God, and he will give it to you. He will not rebuke you for asking. But when you ask him, be sure that your faith is in God alone. Do not waver, for a person with divided loyalty is as unsettled as a wave of the sea that is blown and tossed by the wind (James 1:5-6 NLT).

The LORD will guide you continually,
    giving you water when you are dry
    and restoring your strength.
You will be like a well-watered garden,
    like an ever-flowing spring.
(Isaiah 58:11 NLT)

Do not be wise in your own eyes;
Fear the LORD and depart from evil.
It will be health to your flesh,
And strength to your bones.
(Proverbs 3:7-8)

You guide me with your counsel,
    leading me to a glorious destiny.
(Psalm 73:24 NLT)

SCRIPTURAL AFFIRMATIONS FOR MORAL, RELATIONAL, FINANCIAL, AND HEALTH DECISIONS

Moral Decisions

Integrity and honesty protect me, for I put my hope in You (Psalm 25:21).

I fear the Lord and judge with integrity, for the Lord my God does not tolerate perverted justice, partiality, or the taking of bribes (2 Chronicles 19:7).

I have a covenant with my eyes not to look with lust at a young woman (Job 31:1).

I am blessed and undefiled in my way because I walk in the law of the Lord (Psalm 119:1).

I run from sexual sin. No other sin so clearly affects me because sexual immorality is a sin against my own body (1 Corinthians 6:18).

I am a virtuous wife. My worth is far above rubies. The heart of my husband can safely trust me so that he will have no lack of gain. I will do him good and not evil all the days of my life (Proverbs 31:10-12).

I am an excellent wife and the crown of my husband. I will not cause him shame and be like decay in his bones (Proverbs 12:4).

I follow righteousness and mercy and therefore find life, righteousness, and honor (Proverbs 21:21).

Righteousness delivers me. I will not be caught by the unfaithfulness of lust (Proverbs 11:6).

I keep away from the immoral woman, from the smooth tongue of a promiscuous woman. I do not lust for her beauty, not do I let her coy glances seduce me (Proverbs 6:25).

I drink water from my own well, and share my love only with my wife. I do not spill the water of my springs in the streets by having sex with another. It is reserved just for her, and I do not share it with strangers (Proverbs 5:15-17).

I do not accept bribes, for a bribe blinds the discerning and perverts the words of the righteous (Exodus 23:8).

No temptation has overtaken me except what is common to everyone; but God is faithful, and will not allow me to be tempted beyond what I can bear, but with the temptation will also make the way of escape, that I may be able to endure it (1 Corinthians 10:13).

Relational Decisions

As the elect of God, holy and beloved, I put on tender mercies, kindness, humility, meekness, longsuffering; bearing with others, and forgiving others, if I have a complaint against another; even as Christ forgave me, so I forgive also (Colossians 3:12-13).

My discretion makes me slow to anger, and it is to my glory to overlook a transgression (Proverbs 19:11).

I do not become unequally yoked together with unbelievers because righteousness has no fellowship with lawlessness. And light has no communion with darkness (2 Corinthians 6:14).

I do not look out only for my interests, but I take an interest in others too (Philippians 2:4).

The heart of my husband safely trusts me, so he will have no lack of gain (Proverbs 31:11).

I do not deprive my spouse sexually, except with his or her consent for a certain length of time that we may give ourselves to fasting and prayer.

And then we come together again so that Satan does not tempt us because of our lack of self-control (1 Corinthians 7:5).

As iron sharpens iron, so I sharpen the countenance of my friend (Proverbs 27:17).

I love my neighbor as myself. Because love does no wrong to others, it fulfills the requirements of God's law (Romans 13:9-10).

I am a companion of all who fear God and of those who keep His precepts (Psalm 119:63).

My soft answers turn away wrath and stir up no anger (Proverbs 15:1).

Hatred stirs up strife, but my love covers all sins (Proverbs 10:12).

Love is patient and kind; love does not envy; love does not parade itself, it is not proud; it does not behave rudely, does not seek its own, is not provoked, thinks no evil; love does not rejoice in iniquity but rejoices in the truth; it bears all things, believes all things, hopes all things, endures all things. Love never fails (1 Corinthians 13:4-8).

Financial Decisions

I acknowledge the Lord in all my ways and He directs my paths (Proverbs 3:6).

The Lord teaches me to profit and leads me in the way I should go (Isaiah 48:17).

I listen to sound advice for plans fail for lack of counsel, but with many advisers they succeed (Proverbs 15:22).

Integrity guides me for I am an upright person (Proverbs 11:3).

My heavenly Father wishes that I prosper in all things and be in good health even as my soul prospers (3 John 2).

God opens doors for me that no man can shut (Revelation 3:7).

Because I am in right standing with the Lord, He surrounds me with favor like a shield (Psalm 5:12).

I am not anxious about anything, but in everything by prayer and supplication, with thanksgiving, I let my requests be made known to God. And His peace, which surpasses all understanding, guards my heart and mind through Christ Jesus (Philippians 4:6-7).

I do not team up with those who are unbelievers, for righteousness cannot be in partnership with wickedness and light cannot live with darkness (2 Corinthians 6:14).

The Lord gives me the ability to produce wealth, and so establishes His covenant in the earth (Deuteronomy 8:18).

God is enriching me in every way so that I can always be generous (2 Corinthians 9:11).

Because I am a faithful tither, God pours me out a blessing that I don't have room enough to receive. He rebukes the devourer and keeps him from destroying the fruit of my labor (Malachi 3:10-11).

I am faithful over a few things; therefore, God makes me ruler over many (Matthew 25:21).

I meditate in God's Word day and night so that I may do all that is written in it; thereby, I make my way prosperous and I have good success (Joshua 1:8).

Health Decisions

God's desire for me is to prosper in all things and be in good health, just as my soul prospers (3 John 2).

My peaceful heart leads to a healthy body (Proverbs 14:30).

Kind words are like honey—sweet to my soul and healthy for my body (Proverbs 16:24).

A merry heart is good medicine, but a broken spirit dries up my bones (Proverbs 17:22).

I will wait on the Lord, and He shall renew my strength. I shall mount up with wings like eagles, I shall run and not be weary, I shall walk and not faint (Isaiah 40:31).

But He was wounded for my transgressions; He was bruised for my iniquities. The chastisement for my peace was upon Him, and by His stripes I am healed (Isaiah 53:5).

I am not wise in my own eyes. I fear the Lord and depart from evil. Therefore, it is health to my flesh and strength to my bones (Proverbs 3:7-8).

Because I give attention to Your words and listen to what You say and do not let them depart from my eyes, but keep them in my heart, they are life to me and health to my flesh (Proverbs 4:20-22).

Lord, Your discipline for me is good, for it leads to life and health. You restore my health and allow me to live (Isaiah 38:16).

I am not one whose words pierce like a sword; my tongue is wise and promotes health (Proverbs 12:18).

Bodily exercise profits me a little, but godliness is profitable for me in all things, having promise in the life that now is and in the one to come (1 Timothy 4:8).

My tongue brings healing and is a tree of life, but a deceitful tongue crushes the spirit (Proverbs 15:4).

When I cry out to God, He will heal me (Psalm 30:2).

The Lord heals my broken heart and binds up all my wounds (Psalm 147:3).

SURVEY RESULTS SUMMARY

Question: What is the dumbest type of decision you have ever made? (*Dumb* is defined as the failure to use sound judgment and forethought in light of the circumstances and possible consequences.) Select only ONE category.

Answer Options	Response Percent	Response Count
Spiritual/Moral	15.0 percent	36
Relationship	42.5 percent	102
Financial/Professional	39.6 percent	95
Physical/Health	2.9 percent	7
TOTAL	100.0 percent	**240**

NOTES

Introduction: Decisions, Decisions

1. Andy Pasztor, "Hero Pilot 'Sully' Stars at Safety Hearing," *Wall Street Journal,* June 10, 2009, A-2.

2. *Practices That Related to the Exxon Valdez,* Washington, DC: National Transportation and Safety Board, 18 September 1990, 1-6.

Chapter 1: Dumb Moral Choices

1. "42. Bill Clinton (1993-2001)," www.whitehouse.gov, http://www.whitehouse.gov/about/presidents/williamjClinton (accessed January 11, 2010).

2. Steven Pinker, "The Moral Instinct," New York Times.com, January 13, 2008, http://www.nytimes.com/2008/01/13/magazine/13Psychology-t.html?_r=1&scp=3 (accessed January 12, 2010).

3. Tiger Woods, "Tiger Woods taking hiatus from golf," tigerwoods.com, http://web.tigerwoods.com/news/article/200912117801012/news/ (accessed January 12, 2010).

4. Manuel Velasquez, Claire Andre, Thomas Shanks, S.J., and Michael J. Meyer, "Thinking Ethically: A Framework for Moral Decision Making," scu.edu, 1996, http://www.scu.edu/ethics/publications/iie/v7n1/thinking.html (accessed January 7, 2010).

Chapter 2: Dumb Relational Choices

1. T.D. Jakes, *Before You Do: Making Great Decisions That You Won't Regret* (New York: ATRIA Books, a division of Simon and Schuster, Inc., 2008), 15.

Chapter 3: Dumb Financial and Business Decisions

1. Gracian Mack, "Why Smart People Make Bad Financial Decisions," *Black Enterprise Magazine,* November 1994.

2. http://www.neatorama.com/2008/04/15/the-stupidest-business-decisions-in-history/

Chapter 4: Dumb Health Decisions

1. Lisa Cicciarello Andrews, MEd, RD, LD; "Diet and Nutrition," www.netwellness.org, July 31, 2007, http://www.netwellness.org/healthtopics/diet/ (accessed January 29, 2010).

2. Evelyn L. Fitzwater, DSN, RN, "Healthy Decisions, Healthy Actions," www.netwellness.org, Apr. 2, 2009, http://www.netwellness.org/healthtopics/aging/healthydecisions.cfm# (accessed January 29, 2010).

3. Centers for Disease Control and Prevention, "Chronic Diseases and Health Promotion," www.cdc.gov, Dec. 17, 2009, http://www.cdc.gov/chronicdisease/overview/index.htm (accessed January 29, 2010).

4. "Scanning the Statistics on Smoking," www.dummies.com, 2010, http://www.dummies.com/how-to/content/scanning-the-statistics-on-smoking.html (accessed January 28, 2010).

5. Centers for Disease Control and Prevention, "Chronic Diseases and Health Promotion," www.cdc.gov, December 17, 2009.

6. AHA Scientific Position, "Cigarette Smoking and Cardiovascular Diseases," www.americanheart.org, http://www.americanheart.org/presenter.jhtml?identifier=4545 (accessed January 28, 2010).

7. Bill Hendrick, "Smoking Rate Is Declining in U.S.," www.webmd.com, November 13, 2008, http://www.webmd.com/smoking-cessation/news/20081113/smoking-rate-is-declining-in-us (accessed January 28, 2010).

8. Terry Martin, "About Secondhand Smoke: The Effects of Secondhand Smoke on Our Health," www.about.com, updated July 20, 2008, http://quitsmoking.about.com/cs/secondhandsmoke/a/secondhandsmoke.htm (accessed January 30, 2010).

9. http://www.bloodalcohol.info/how-alcohol-affects-the-brain.php (accessed February 3, 2010).

10. "Winston Churchill Quotes," www.brainyquote.com, http://www.brainyquote.com/quotes/quotes/w/winstonchu382960.html (accessed January 28, 2010).

11. Cari Haus, "How Far Did Jesus Walk?" www.Iluvwalking.com, February 28, 2009, http://iluvwalking.com/blog/2009/02/28/how-far-did-jesus-walk/ (accessed January 28, 2010).

12. Des Cummings, Jr., PhD, and Monica Reed, MD, *Creation Health Discovery* (Orlando: Florida Hospital Publishing, 2005), 55.

Chapter 5: Arrested by Anger

1. "Anger, Hostility, and Violent Behavior—Topic Overview," webmd.com, January 18, 2008, http://www.webmd.com/balance/tc/anger-and-hostility-topic-overview (accessed January 5, 2010).

2. Dr. Scott Jakubowski, PhD, "Anger Is Often a Secondary Emotion," thespectrum.com, August 31, 2009, http://www.thespectrum.com/article/20090831/LIFESTYLE/908310313/1024/CUSTOMERSERVICE02 (accessed September 30, 2009).

3. Houston Mitchell, "Serena Williams fined $82,500 and put on probation for U.S. Open tirade," latimes.com, Nov. 30, 2009, http://latimesblogs.latimes.com/sports_blog/2009/12/serena-williams-ap-female-athlete-of-the-year.html (accessed December 30, 2009).

Chapter 6: Fueled by Fear

1. *Dune*, film, directed by David Lynch (Mexico City, Mexico: Universal Pictures, 1984).

2. Caroline Leaf, *Who Switched Off My Brain?* (Switch on Your Brain USA, Inc., 2008), 19-20.

3. Ibid.

4. Gregory Berns, MD, PhD, "In Hard Times, Fear Can Impair Decision-Making," *New York Times*, December 7, 2008, http://www.nytimes.com/2008/12/07/jobs/07pre.html (accessed January 15, 2010).

5. Dwight Bain, "Frozen by the Fear of Wrong Decisions," http://www.cbn.com/finance/bain_wrongdecisions.aspx (accessed January 15, 2010).

Chapter 7: Galvanized by Greed

1. http://www.hoovers.com/company/Enron_Creditors_Recovery_Corp/rfhtri-1.html (accessed January 28, 2009).

2. *New York Times*, June 30, 2009, http://www.nytimes.com/2009/06/30/business/30madoff .html (accessed 1/28/09).

Chapter 8: Injured by Impatience

1. "Could Impatience Be Raising Your Blood Pressure?" WebMD.com, October 22, 2003, http:// www.webmd.com/hypertension-high-blood-pressure/impatience_and_blood_pressure (accessed January 8, 2010).

2. Bob Lancer, "End Impatience Now—Part 1," EzineArticles.com, July 1, 2008 http://ezinearticles .com/?End-Impatience-Now—Part-1&id=1291631 (accessed January 8, 2010).

3. Ibid.

Chapter 11: Lured by Lust

1. http://sportsillustrated.cnn.com/vault/article/magazine/MAG1141820/index.htm

Chapter 12: Prompted by Pride

1. Are You an Egomaniac? Ten Questions with Steven Smith, http://blog.guykawasaki .com/2007/09/are-you-an-egom.html#ixzz0cTPwwpTZ (accessed January 12, 2010).

Chapter 15: Clear Objectives

1. Lewis Carroll, *Alice's Adventures in Wonderland* (New York: Alfred A Knopf, 1984), 89.

2. http://ezinearticles.com/?Decision-Making—The-Importance-Of-A-Clear-Objective &id=899239 (accessed January 28, 2010).

Chapter 16: Concrete Information

1. www.neatorama.com/2008/04/15/the-stupidest-business-decisions-in-history/

2. Ibid.

3. Jonah Lehrer, *How We Decide* (New York: Houghton Mifflin Harcourt Publishing Co., 2009), 206.

Chapter 17: Contemplation

1. "The Dangers of Hasty Decision-making," *Business Management Daily,* adapted from "The Secrets of Great Decision-Making," Anne Fisher, *Fortune,* http://www.businessmanagementdaily .com/articles/13438/1/The-dangers-of-hasty-decision-making/Page1.html

Chapter 18: Counsel

1. Jillian Downer, "What Is a Caucus?" http://www.ehow.com/about_4672138_caucus.html (accessed January 13, 2010).

2. John P. Kotter, *Leading Change* (Boston, MA: Harvard Business School Press, 1996), 6-7.

3. Miguel Bustillo and Geoffrey A. Fowler, "Sears Scrambles Online for a Lifeline," January 16, 2010, http://online.wsj.com/article/SB10001424052748704362004575000980281250618. html (accessed January 15, 2010).

Chapter 19: Creativity

1. http://en.wikipedia.org/wiki/Thinking_outside_the_box

2. Avis Rent a Car, "A History of One of the World's Most Recognized Taglines: We Try Harder," http://www.avis.com.cy/en/mqavis/We_try_harder.html (accessed September 24, 2009).

3. "Advertising: Trying Harder," *Time*, July 24, 1964, http://www.time.com/time/magazine/article/0,9171,939058,00.html (accessed September 24, 2009).

4. http://www.articlesbase.com/leadership-articles/bad-business-decisions-and-famous-quotes-451168.html

5. Ibid.

6. http://finapps.forbes.com/finapps/jsp/finance/compinfo/CIAtAGlance.jsp?tkr=AAPL

Chapter 20: Courage

1. Sandra Ford Walston, "Courage Leadership: How to Claim Your Courage and Help Others Do the Same," www.bnet.com, August 2003, http://findarticles.com/p/articles/mi_m0MNT/is_8_57/ai_106523131/ (accessed January 19, 2010).

2. Joel Michael Evans. *Mastering the Art of Decision-Making* (Borough of Manhattan Community College of The City University of New York); http://www.youtube.com/watch?v=zN6n8FKvLW0 (accessed January 20, 2010).

3. Andrew Pollack, "Apple Computer Entrepreneur's Rise and Fall," *New York Times,* September 19, 1985, http://www.nytimes.com/1985/09/19/business/apple-computer-entrepreneur-s-rise-and-fall.html (accessed January 19, 2010).

4. "Steve Jobs," http://www.answers.com/topic/steve-jobs (accessed January 20, 2010).

5. Simran Khurana, "Billy Graham Quotes," http://quotations.about.com/od/stillmorefamouspeople/a/BillyGraham1.htm (accessed January 20, 2010).

Chapter 21: Clean Conscience

1. Kenneth E. Goodpaster, "Conscience and Corporate Culture," www.thechiefexecutive.com, December 19, 2006, http://www.the-chiefexecutive.com/features/feature833/ (accessed January 26, 2010).

2. Alan S. L. Long, "The Work of Our Conscience," October 1997, http://www.vtaide.com/blessing/conscience.htm (accessed January 25, 2010).

How to Contact the Authors

Website: www.SmartPeopleDumbChoices.com

For speaking engagements, please contact the authors at:

Deborah Smith Pegues
P.O. Box 56382
Los Angeles, CA 90056
323.293.5861

Email: ddpegues@sbcglobal.net

Website: www.ConfrontingIssues.com

Ricky Temple
P. O. Box 15789
Savannah, GA 31416
912.927.8601 ext. 212

Email: Rickytemple@OvercomingbyFaith.org
Website: www.RickyTemple.com